CONTENTS

APPENDICES

THE
JEWEL HOUSE

An Account of the Many Romances
Connected with the Royal Regalia
Together with Sir Gilbert Talbot's
Account of Colonel Blood's Plot
Here reproduced for the first Time

BY MAJOR-GENERAL
SIR GEORGE YOUNGHUSBAND

K.C.M.G., K.C.I.E., C.B.

KEEPER OF THE JEWEL HOUSE

ILLUSTRATED IN COLOUR, ETC.

HERBERT JENKINS LIMITED
3 YORK STREET ST. JAMES'S
LONDON S.W.1 ✺ ✺ MCMXXI

ILLUSTRATIONS

THE JEWEL HOUSE

CHAPTER I

THE JEWEL HOUSE

When kings began to reign—The Crown of the King of the Ammon-
ites—A Crown weighing 125 lbs.—The Treasure House of
Kings—Egbert the first King of England—His regalia—King
Alfred's Crown—Edward the Confessor's Crown and Staff and
Ring—The Crown Jewels first placed in Westminster Abbey—
Henry III removes them to the Tower of London—The Jewel
Chamber in the White Tower—The Jewel House in the reign of
Queen Elizabeth—The Martin Tower turned into the Jewel
House by Charles II—The word "Bolleyn" on the wall—
Northumberland and Heriot prisoners there—A slender guard
and the result—Colonel Blood fails in his attempt on the Crown
—Northumberland's ghost—Narrow escape from fire of the
Jewel House—Removal of Crown Jewels to the Wakefield
Tower—Its former history—Origin of name—The murder of
Henry VI in this tower—The young Princes buried in the base-
ment—The lesson from St. Patrick's Jewels—King Edward VII
makes the Jewels secure—The tantalized burglar—The German
lady and the Kaiser's hopes—The Jewels in the Great War—
Their narrow escapes—Their removal till the end of the War—
Return to the Tower—Their wonderful adventures as recorded.

WHEN Kings first began to reign on earth
they wore on their heads and carried in
their hands the emblems of royalty.
To give them dignity, the seats they
occupied were raised and glorified and became
thrones. Thousands of years ago the crown became

the mark of sovereignty, for did not Saul fight his last battle wearing his crown, and with the bracelet on his arm ? Whilst the prophet Samuel in his book records that the crown of the King of the Ammonites, taken in battle by King David, was of pure gold, studded with precious stones. The prophet also commits himself so far as to add that this crown weighed one talent. Perhaps in this detail we may make allowance for Eastern hyperbole, a talent being equivalent to 125 lb., or the weight of two fair-sized portmanteaux. It is not reasonable to assume that even the most muscular King would with equanimity thus handicap himself whilst waging war. The throne of Solomon has become historic, made, we are told, of ivory overlaid with gold with a lion standing on each side, and twelve lions guarding the sides of each of the six steps that led up to it. As the value and number of kingly emblems increased, it became necessary to deposit them when not in use in a place of security strongly guarded, which came to be known as the Treasure House of the King. In ancient days it was not unusual to place the Regalia in some holy place, such as a church or cathedral, where the sanctity of the building was held to be an additional safeguard ; but more usually it would be kept with the King in his castle.

Egbert, the first King of England, was crowned nearly eleven hundred years ago, in A.D. 827, and

King George V, the present King of England, is his direct descendant. The English monarchy is the oldest in Europe, and the English Royal Family had a longer pedigree than that of any European potentate, even before the Great War. The kingly emblems in King Egbert's days were few and of no great value, probably nothing more than a crown and a sceptre. The crown of King Alfred was made of gold wire, and was, when broken up and melted down by the Commonwealth, valued only at £238 10s. 0d. Edward the Confessor, besides a crown, had a staff or long sceptre, a replica of which is now amongst the Crown Jewels. He also had a Coronation ring set with a large and very fine sapphire, which same sapphire may be seen in the cross paté on top of King George V's State Crown.

As the Crown Jewels increased in number and value, the King ceased to carry them about with him on all occasions, and they were handed over to the safe keeping of the Abbot and monks of Westminster. In Westminster Abbey can still be pointed out the Chapel of the Pix, where the regal emblems were kept. It is not improbable that Edward the Confessor inaugurated this manner of safeguarding the Regalia when not in use, and his successors for two hundred years followed his example. But though Westminster Abbey proved a sure sanctuary against robbers and marauders from the outer world, unfortunately within the sacred walls were those inured to sanctity, and who were by no means indisposed to profit in so obvious and mundane a matter as disposing of the Crown Jewels. Probably the Treasure Chamber was rarely inspected or visited, and as the monks themselves were the guardians, inconvenient inquiries might easily be disposed of, unless and until certain portions of the Regalia were required for the King's personal use. It was doubtless some such demand which led to the discovery that the Treasure Chamber had been broken into and some of the Regalia had disappeared.

The chief regal emblems, such as the Crown and Sceptre, had been transferred to the Tower by Henry III, but the lesser yet very valuable pieces of plate were still at Westminster. The theft was brought home to a monk named Alexandre de Pershore, who had sold the plate to a travelling merchant named Richard de Podelicote. As a result the Abbot Wenlock and forty-eight monks were tried and sentenced to two years' imprisonment in the Tower. This was in the reign of Edward I, and as a result the King decided that Westminster Abbey was not altogether a safe place for any portion of so valuable a collection of plate and jewelry, and ordered it all to be transferred to the Tower of London. An official Keeper of the Regalia, whose duty it was to guard and have sole custody of the Jewels, had already been appointed by Henry III, and henceforth a divided control ceased.

From that day, some seven hundred years ago, the grey old walls of the Tower of London have been the outer casing of the casket which has contained the Crown Jewels of thirty-two Kings and Queens of England. The Jewels were probably first placed in the White Tower, that being the central keep of the Tower of London, itself then, and for many centuries after, the strongest fortress in England. On the north side of the crypt of St John's Chapel, which is in the White Tower, there is a small chamber with only one entrance and with no windows. This chamber, which some erroneous person for long marked as the cell of Sir Walter Raleigh,[1] would in those days have been an ideal place for the safe storage of the Regalia. It is not only an inner sanctuary, but also it was guarded without all round by soldiers and by battlements. A monk might pilfer the plate, but he had to get it past the soldiers and out of the fortress to profit by his prowess. In this sanctuary, in the crypt of St. John's Chapel, the royal emblems and plate may well have remained for several reigns, and perhaps some centuries, but as the Regalia increased in quantity these restricted quarters would have been found too small to conveniently and suitably house them. Thus we find in an accurate survey of the

---

[1] It is very clear from all historical records that Sir Walter Raleigh was never imprisoned in the White Tower, so that a misguiding notice in the crypt might well be removed.

Tower of London, made in 1597, in the reign of Queen Elizabeth, that a special Jewel House had been built outside of and adjoining the south face of the White Tower. This Jewel House was a long low building with a flat, castellated roof, whilst at the western end was a tall turret. There were two entrances, one through the turret and one in the middle of the south wall. The building was evidently one of two storeys, as two tiers of windows are shown, with two lights on each floor.

The Regalia remained in this Jewel House through the reigns of James I and Charles I, but with the tragic death of this last unhappy monarch the need for a Jewel House disappeared, for by orders of the Parliament all regal emblems were broken up, destroyed, or sold for what they would fetch. Unused and uncared for, the old Jewel House fell into decay and disrepair, and became no longer a place of safe keeping. Thus when the Restoration came and Charles II ascended the throne of his forefathers, a new Treasure House had to be found. The place fixed upon was the Martin Tower, which forms the north-east bastion of the inner ballium wall of the Tower of London. Who Martin was, or why this tower was named after him, has escaped all researches, but it is of interest to note that the Middle Tower was at one time called the Martin Tower, and the inference seems to be that some well-known personage who had long lived in the

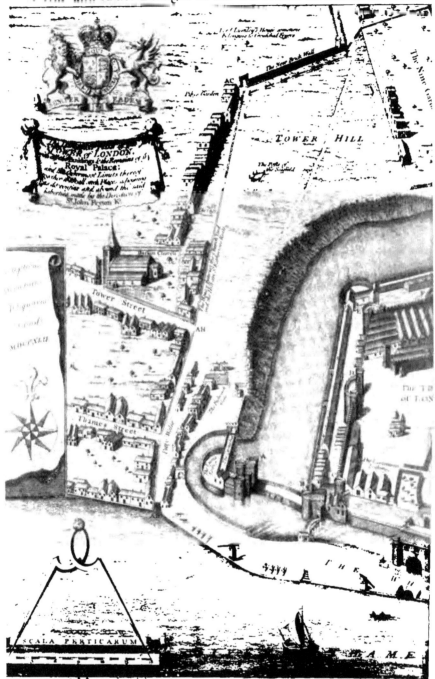

Merchant Taylors Alms Houses

Hog Lane

The Citye's Ditch

The place where the Crosse stood

EAST SMITH FIELD

East Smith Field

A Note of the Liberties of the Tower as it appears in the Lease from 17 Hen. VIII

The Several Towers.

A The Middle Tower
B The Tower at the Gate
C The Bell Tower
D Beauchamp Tower
E Develin Tower
F Flint Tower
G Bowyer Tower
H Brick Tower
I Mint Tower
K Constable Tower
L Broad Arrow Tower
M Salt Tower
N Well Tower
O The Tower leading to the Iron Gate
P The Entrance of the Iron Gate
Q The Cradle Tower
R The Lanthorn Tower
S The Hall Tower
T The Bloody Tower
V S. Thomas Tower
W Caesar or White Tower
X Cole Harbour
Y Wardrobe Tower

MOORE

Jewel House

The Queenes Lodgings

Jewell House

The Hall Lodging

The Privy Garden

Boundaries of the Liberties

AB The House at the Water Gate called Iron House
AC The Parish Church Wall called the Bulwark Gate
AD The City Wall at the N. by the New Garden
AE The Place where the Posterne Tower was
AF Hog Lane End
AG The Highway and the Stone corner House
AH The End of Tower Street
AI The Stairs without the East End Well Tower

Tower of London first occupied quarters in the Middle Tower and afterwards those in the Martin Tower, and that on his death from long association his name attached itself to his last residence.

When Charles II came to the throne, all the regal emblems, such as the Crown, the Sceptre, and the Orb, had to be remade to replace those destroyed by the Commonwealth, whilst the royal plate had also to be renewed. Naturally, therefore, it took some time for the Regalia to arrive at its former excellence and value; during the early years of the reign it could be easily housed, and was apparently not considered to be of sufficient importance to be guarded by soldiers. It was thus placed in the lower floor of the Martin Tower, which in former reigns had been used more frequently as a place of imprisonment for the more important or more affluent prisoners. Inscribed on one of the walls inside is the word "Bolleyn," which for long was held to be the mark of Queen Anne Boleyn, and as such held up as proof that the unhappy lady was imprisoned in the Martin Tower. But a closer examination of the records of those days shows conclusively that the Queen was never imprisoned in that particular tower; on the other hand, during this examination it became sufficiently clear that her brother, George Boleyn, Viscount Rochford, was probably a prisoner here, and the inscription may very possibly have been carved by

B

him. Another mark of an old prisoner in the
Martin Tower is the sundial on the south wall,
ascribed to Heriot the astronomer, who together
with Henry Percy, Earl of Northumberland, known
as " Hotspur," was for long a prisoner here.[1]

The sole guardian of King Charles' new Crown
Jewels in the Martin Tower, unaided by sentries or
yeomen, was an old man named Talbot Edwards,
then nearly eighty years of age, who was Assistant
Keeper of the Jewel House under Sir Gilbert Talbot.
Edwards and his family occupied the upper storeys
of the Martin Tower, but Sir Gilbert Talbot lived
chiefly at the Palace at Whitehall, it being one of
his duties to reside always in whichever palace
the King happened to be occupying from time to
time. The chamber in which the Jewels were
placed was semi-circular in shape with one door,
and with very thick walls. In the outer or thickest
wall was made, or already existed, a recess which,
when a cross-wired door had been added, formed a
cupboard, the front of which was open to view.
This arrangement was made not only so that the
Jewels might easily be inspected, but also because it
was one of the perquisites of the Assistant Keeper
to show the Crown Jewels to visitors for such fees
as he could inveigle out of them. There were no
guards either of soldiers or yeomen on the Regalia ;

[1] This Henry Percy, "Hotspur," appears as an early ancestor
in the genealogy of the Younghusband family.

THE JEWEL HOUSE BY THE MARTIN TOWER, 1815

which fact, becoming known to the notorious Colonel Blood, that worthy with two accomplices attempted to steal the Crown Jewels, as is recorded in due course.[1]

The attempt, though it very nearly succeeded, failed rather through good fortune than from any wise precaution. It, however, brought to notice the insecure manner in which the Regalia were kept, much as the theft of the St. Patrick's Jewels in Edward VII's reign drew similar attention, and it was decided in due course to build a new Jewel House specially constructed to ensure security. The site chosen was just below the Martin Tower on its western side, between that tower and the then existing Armoury. This site was not an ideal one, so that quite early after its occupation reports were made that the new Jewel House was liable to be endangered by sparks from the chimneys or furnaces of the Armoury, which was only a few feet away. A guard of soldiers was now placed on the building, and yeomen warders were detailed, or hired by the Assistant Keeper, to aid him in his duties. The guard furnished a double sentry on this post, which was afterwards reduced to a single sentry. But this sentry declared that he nightly saw the ghost of the Earl of Northumberland walking up and down what is now known as Northumberland's walk, a narrow beat along the

[1] See Chapter XI.

edge of the ramparts running each side of the Martin Tower. When one sentry had seen the ghost, others also were ready to declare that they also had seen it, so that as time went on and the superstition grew, the post became decidedly unpopular amongst the soldiers, whilst some even refused to go on it alone. The sentry was therefore again doubled, and the Earl and his midnight walks faded away into the mists of antiquity.

As illustrating how persons who are determined to see ghosts may succeed in doing so, this is a very useful incident. This Henry Percy, Earl of Northumberland, known as " Hotspur " from his fiery temper, who for thirteen years was imprisoned in the Martin Tower, lived there in ease and such comfort as wealth could in those days command, and eventually left under a salute from the great guns of the Tower, a guard of honour, and an escort to Northumberland House, at the head of what is now Northumberland Avenue. There was no tragedy whatever about his long sojourn in the Tower. His father, however, another Henry Percy, Earl of Northumberland, was without doubt murdered in the Bloody Tower, so that if the Northumberland ghost had taken his nightly walks about the Bloody Tower there would have been some sensible connection. Evidently the ignorant soldiery of the day mixed up the two Earls of Northumberland, and imagined the wrong one nightly pacing the portion of the ramparts, which he had probably never even seen in his lifetime, for the Martin Tower and the Bloody Tower are on opposite sides of the fortress and quite invisible one from the other.

Another ghost sworn to in the Martin Tower is that of Queen Anne Boleyn. A worthy warder a century or so ago under sworn testimony gave an account of how Anne Boleyn had appeared at suppertime, in the form of a bluish grey column, like smoke in a glass tube. How exactly the Queen was recognised in this disguise is not stated, but the main point is that Queen Anne Boleyn was never imprisoned in the Martin Tower. She went straight to the Lieutenants' Lodgings and from there to her execution. As has been already mentioned, however, her brother, George Boleyn, Viscount Rochford, was undoubtedly a prisoner in the Martin Tower, and on one of the inner walls is roughly engraved the name " Bolleyn." History and records and tradition doubtless became somewhat mixed as the centuries passed, so that warder after warder, on taking over these quarters, heard from his predecessor that the engraving had been made by Queen Anne Boleyn. A bowl of punch, and a lively imagination, would produce the rest of this ghost story.

Inside the new Jewel House a strong cage was constructed, through the bars of which by light of dim lanterns the Crown Jewels could be seen at certain hours by those who had passes, and were prepared to pay a fee for the same. That the tremors of those who feared danger from fire were not unfounded eventually proved only too true. In 1843 the Armoury, which as mentioned was only a few feet from the Jewel House, caught fire and was burnt to the ground, placing the Crown Jewels in most imminent peril. That they escaped severe damage, if not destruction, was due to the great presence of mind, ready resource, and courage of a Sergeant, who broke into the Jewel House, and aided by yeomen bundled the precious articles without ceremony out on to the parade ground. Though thus hastily cast forth, and in spite of the crowd and confusion, nothing was lost or injured. It would be gratifying to be able to record that the hero of this adventure received some notable recognition of the service he had rendered. Truth, however, impels the confession that the deed was at the time eclipsed by the great tragedy of the burning down of the ancient Armoury, a building several centuries old with many historic associations. Later, when this conspicuous service came to light, the ardour of recompense had grown cold.

The next, and present, abode of the Crown Jewels became the Wakefield Tower, one of the lesser towers on the inner ballium wall, adjoining the Bloody Tower and facing the Traitors' Gate. The origin of the name has been a subject of some

THE JEWEL HOUSE IN THE TOWER OF LONDON

Campbell Gray photo

discussion. For many years, indeed for some centuries, the Wakefield Tower was held to have been so named because the prisoners taken at the battle of Wakefield were therein imprisoned. But further examination shows that this tower was never used as a prison, nor could it have contained the number of prisoners supposed to have been incarcerated in it. Moreover, there is some evidence that the name was given to this tower long before the battle of Wakefield. A more reliable conclusion is that it was named after William de Wakefield, one of the King's Clerks, who was appointed to hold custody of the Exchanges in the Tower in 1344, and very possibly had his office in part of this building.

In ancient days the Wakefield Tower, then named the Hall, formed the entrance to the Royal Palace, which fell into decay during the reign of Queen Elizabeth. She having been a prisoner in the Tower as a Princess, had conceived such a horror for the place that when she became Queen she refused to live there. In previous reigns the King or Queen always lived in the Tower before their Coronation, and thence proceeded in state, preceded by the Knights of the Bath, to Westminster. In the Wakefield Tower is still a small chapel or oratory which was used as a private place of devotion by the Monarch when in residence at the Palace. In this little chapel, whilst kneeling at his prayers, Henry VI was murdered by Richard of Gloucester.

A narrow, winding stair, some of the steps now so worn with age as to be hardly safe, leads down from the adjacent Bloody Tower to the basement. Down these steps the bodies of the two young Princes who were murdered there were dragged, and hastily buried in the basement of the Wakefield Tower. Here they lay for five days when Richard of Gloucester, by whose order they had been murdered, made the somewhat superfluous discovery that the bodies were not buried in consecrated ground. They were hastily dug up and buried close to the south wall of the White Tower; and being there more or less under the shadow of St. John's Chapel, were considered suitably interred. The Constable of the Tower, Sir Robert Brackenbury, was the only person who knew the secret, and he died with it, being shortly afterwards killed at the battle of Bosworth. It was not till the reign of Charles II that the remains of the two little Princes were accidentally found, and by order of the King removed to Westminster and buried there.

The walls of the Wakefield Tower are eight feet thick, and there is only one entrance, whilst the windows are heavily barred. In these more or less practical days, however, reliance is not placed solely on solid walls, or even on sentries and yeomen, to keep the Crown Jewels in safety.

After the St. Patrick's Jewels had been stolen in Dublin, King Edward VII determined that the Crown Jewels of England should be placed, as far as human prescience could devise, beyond the power of anyone to tamper with them. The most expert mechanical and scientific genuises, with Messrs. Chubb at their head, were called into consultation, and the result was the invention of the present octagonal-shaped steel casement furnished with steel bars.

It is naturally not allowable to mention what the mechanical safeguards are, but the inexpert or indeed expert thief may certainly count on being guillotined or electrocutioned if he makes the attempt to emulate Colonel Blood's adventure. It has been a source of some amusement to the warders to watch known burglars—for admission to view the Crown Jewels is open to all His Majesty's subjects, not excluding burglars—with their faces flattened against the bars thinking, thinking, thinking, how possibly they could get hold of these priceless gems. One indeed, with a deep resigned sigh, was heard to mutter, " Gor' blimy it ain't to be done ! " So we may hope for the best. Not only, however, are the Crown Jewels guarded by all the resources of science, but soldiers, yeomen warders, and policemen keep watch over them night and day.

Just before the War, amongst other visitors was a German lady, who looked long at the Jewels and

carefully examined the steel encasement in which
they are exhibited. Then she went back to one of the
yeomen on duty and remarked, "You may think
those Jewels very wonderful and very wonderfully
guarded, but do not be surprised if I say that they
will soon belong to our Kaiser." The yeoman was
so taken aback that he did not know what to say,
yet made perhaps a better reply than much forethought might have supplied. He said, "I don't
think so, madam. Pass along, please." This old
yeoman was in the Cameron Highlanders at the
Relief of Lucknow.

During the Great War the Germans in their
first daylight raids made a special target of
the Tower of London, clearly marked as it lay
below on the banks of another clear landmark,
the Thames. That their efforts to hit it were not
more successful was a matter of bad luck for them
and good for us, for we had then no anti-aircraft
guns to drive them off. The first bomb just missed
the Tower to the westward, and fell into the dry
moat in the part used by the garrison as their drill
ground. It penetrated six feet of gravel and rubble,
deflecting at a slight angle as it went downward;
then it ran nearly level for four more feet, and
finally turned upwards at an angle and traversed
another eighteen inches. Happily it failed to explode.
When with much caution it was dug out tail first
it was found to measure $4\frac{1}{2}$ ft. The top 22 in.

formed an ordinary percussion shell, such as is fired
by field artillery; the rest of the bomb consisted of
a brass cylinder filled with a yellow powder. This
powder, though perhaps intended for purely incen-
diary purposes, was doubtless intentionally also of a
highly poisonous nature. So poisonous indeed was it
that those who touched it were afflicted for months
with a species of blood poisoning, which seriously
affected their health and produced a painful and irrita-
ting skin disease. Indeed, one official was thus affected
who had not to his knowledge even touched the
infected portions of one of these bombs; he had
merely stood close to where a wall was plastered
with the yellow powder from an exploded bomb,
whilst a strong wind happened to blow grains of it
in his face. He came out with the same eruption,
though in a less virulent form than the one who had
actual man-handled a piece of the bomb.

This bomb will probably be found in the Imperial
War Museum, but it seemed to us that the gods
intervened to get it there. When the bomb had been
dug out urgent messages arrived by telephone and
otherwise that no one was to meddle with the
blamed thing (I am not sure of the exact wording)
till an expert from the Ordnance Department arrived.
Arrive he did, and how he ever departed, except in a
ring of smoke and glory, puzzles us still. He took
up the live shell, and directing everybody to stand
well clear, a hundred yards or so away, for fear of

accidents, he proceeded to unscrew the percussion fuze at the head of the bomb. This in itself is a delicate operation even for an expert. Apparently the head would not unscrew, but the expert nothing dismayed started hammering and forcing it in a manner which made mere amateurs tremble not only for the intrepid expert, but for the ancient walls of the Tower of London. Finally this philosophic warrior decided that unaided he could not unscrew the head, so he demanded that a taxi should be sent for. Into the taxi entered the gallant gunner and the bomb, and apparently they arrived safely somewhere, for in spite of the censorship, we should probably have heard if he had not.

The second bomb again just missed the Tower, this time to the eastward. Most unfortunately, however, it hit the Royal mint, which stands just across the road. This bomb did the mint, as such, no harm worth mentioning, nothing to interfere with work being carried on as usual, but it so happened that it fell close to where a goodly number of workmen, not actually working at the moment, were assembled, and caused forty-four casualties. One small boy looking upwards was heard to say, " Why, it looks like a bird," and the next second he was himself up and out in the blue of heaven.

The third bomb hit the railings to the north of the Tower, and whilst doing no harm whatever to it caused some damage outside. A couple of horses drawing a van were killed, and many windows in Postern Row were broken. The effect was very much that of a shrapnel shell bursting, indeed there probably was a shrapnel fixed at the head of the bomb, as in the case of the first bomb mentioned. The bullets from this shrapnel shell had sufficient force to make clean round holes through stout iron railings, whilst naturally they went through windows and doors as through paper. Against the flimsiest walls they were of no avail, leaving only pit marks and knocking off plaster.

The fourth bomb I chanced to see myself. I was sitting at my writing-desk, which is near one of the south windows of St. Thomas' Tower, and to be quite exact was writing a note to a lady thanking her for a book she had kindly sent me. There being a good deal of din in the skies, though little enough to one who was just back from the War, I happened to glance out on the river. At that exact moment, only a few yards away, something from the skies fell splosh into the river, and a column of water some six or seven feet high demonstrated the fact. That was the closest shot which the Germans made at the Crown Jewels of England. The total casualties to the credit of this attack on the Tower were one pigeon, which probably had a weak heart and died of shell-shock, and one pane of window broken in the Jewel House.

After these narrow escapes it was decided that

it would be wiser not to chance further risks, and to place the Regalia in a less exposed place than the Tower of London. Consequently the Jewel House was closed for repairs, so to speak, and the Crown Jewels were removed elsewhere. The wonderful stories evolved by the more emotional persons over this ordinary precaution were not without interest. One inspired person mentioned, that from certain information he had received a castle in Cornwall had been secretly acquired and that the Jewels had been taken there by special train at dead of night. He added that in front of the Jewel train, and behind it, were two other trains full of troops, police, detectives, machine-guns, and what not.

Another very astute gentleman had secured the exclusive information, which he imparted with a knowing smile as between two conspirators, that for the past eight months a deep and secret vault lined throughout with concrete had been excavated at Bath, and that the Jewels were now safely deposited there. The sole ground for this rumour rested on the undoubted fact that eight months before the Keeper of the Jewel House had been at Bath, and there, by way of camouflage doubtless had undergone a course of the waters. Another equally knowing individual, a son of Israel, said that he knew for certain that the Jewels were in Cumberland, the slender thread on which this rumour hung being due to the fact that the late Keeper of the Jewel

House, Sir Arthur Wynne, had now settled in Cumberland. When these stories were told it was incumbent to smile in rather an embarrassed manner, as one found out in doing a fatuous thing, and the informants generally departed feeling like an embodiment of Fouché and Sherlock Holmes. It was only necessary to add, " Please do not mention your suspicions to anyone, it might get into the papers," to ensure that it got anyway as far as the Censor.

But these rumours as to where the Jewels were, and how they got there, were nothing to the brilliant stories of their return, which an unfettered, an uncensored press could now make public. One of the more emotional ran : " At dead of night two officers of the Grenadier Guards dressed in frock coats and with silk hats, and each carrying an automatic pistol, drove up to the secret hiding-place in a closed motor-car. With them were two detectives also in civilian clothes but with bowler hats ; they too were armed with automatic pistols. Beside the military chauffeur, dressed in khaki sat another soldier with his loaded rifle at the ' present.' In a few seconds the Crown Jewels were transferred from the secret strong-room to the car by the two officers, whilst the detectives stood tensely at the alert, their pistols cocked. In a few minutes all was ready, and the car sharply wheeling on the gravel drive sped at the rate of forty miles an hour to the Tower of London."

Which is all very nice and lurid, but as a matter of fact the whole process of taking the Jewels away and returning them to the Tower was much more simply accomplished and was not nearly so dramatic. It is now no longer a secret that a royal car drove into the Tower of London and up to the Jewel House. Into it the more important and valuable portions of the Regalia, already packed in their own cases, were handed. It was all a matter of a few minutes, and then the car drove away to Windsor Castle, and there deposited the Jewels in a secure place. The return journey at the end of the War was equally simply and effectively accomplished. Nor was there probably any officer of the Grenadier Guards, with or without a silk hat, nearer than the far dim horizon of Flanders. Naturally, however, the Crown Jewels do not travel without very careful precautions, and these, those who trembled for them may be assured, were fully taken.

During their absence from the Tower some of the cases had somehow got rather damp and mildewy, the sight of which caused the Court Jewellers more than a little anguish. This dampness probably accounts for another brave story, to the effect that the Crown Jewels had been sunk in the river opposite the Tower, and had in this moist retreat been kept for many months.

It is remarkable how wonderfully indiscreet some

ambitious news collectors may become. Information regarding the location or movement of jewels of priceless value may be confided to all and sundry of the honest folks in these realms, but newspapers are bought not only by honest persons, and it is of considerable interest to a professional burglar or jewel thief to be informed exactly how and when he can best make a bid for so great a prize.

Thus we see that throughout the centuries the Jewels have in turn been safeguarded first in Westminster Abbey, then in the White Tower, next in an annexe to the White Tower, after this in the Martin Tower, and then in a special building close to the Martin Tower. Finally, but for a brief sojourn at Windsor Castle during the Great War, in the Wakefield Tower.

c

THE REGALIA IN THE TOWER

THE CROWNS

THE most valuable and important portions of the Regalia, and those which appeal most to the eye and the imagination, are the Royal Crowns. Of these there are three which pertain to the reigning sovereign, whether a King or a Queen. Next there are two crowns and a diadem which pertain to the Queen Consort, when a King is on the throne. And lastly

there is the crown of the eldest son of the King,
who is, if not by right yet at the King's pleasure,
always created Prince of Wales.

The three crowns of the Sovereign are:

(1) St. Edward the Confessor's Crown, or the
    Crown of England.
(2) The Imperial State Crown.
(3) The Imperial Crown of India.

The original crown of Edward the Confessor was
destroyed by the Commonwealth, but on the restoration of Charles II a replica was made, and this is
the crown now to be seen in the Jewel House, and
is the one with which all the Kings and Queens of
England have been crowned since 1661. It was
made of " massie gold " and is of the shape known
as royal in contradistinction to the form described
as imperial. The shape of a Royal crown is familiar
to all from childhood upwards, for it is the crown
which stands on the shield supported by the lion
and the unicorn in the arms of England.

True, the older figure has become somewhat
blurred to the younger generation, since Edward VII
substituted an Imperial Crown for the older shape
on many things, including the Royal mail and
Royal note-paper. This was done of set purpose,
being a sign and portent that the kingdom had
grown into a world-wide empire, greater far and
more rich and populous than any empire that had
existed since the beginning of the world. But the

Crown of England retains its ancient shape. Round the band of this Crown are set at intervals great stones of different colours, red, and blue, and green, and yellow. Above the band stand alternately fleurs-de-lis and crosses patés, from these spring the two golden arches of the Crown, edged all the way with large pearls. These arches are the insignia of a ruling monarch; without them the Crown would remain only a coronet. Where the two arches cross each other they are deeply depressed, and in the hollow thus formed stands a monde or globe of gold. On the monde is fixed a richly jewelled cross with large drop-shaped pearls, pendent from the arms. The weight of this Crown is nearly 5 lbs.

Inside the Crown is the Cap of Maintenance of purple velvet, with an edging of minever to protect the King's head from too hard a contact with solid gold. The original Crown of England, of which, as has been mentioned, this is a copy, is said to have descended century after century from Edward the Confessor, who ascended the throne in 1042. The Vandals of the Commonwealth have much to answer for !

The King's State Crown is more beautiful, and intrinsically of immensely greater value than St. Edward's Crown. It is, however, as a crown comparatively modern, the custom being for each succeeding King or Queen to have their own State Crown made afresh. But the stones that are set in it, of which there are many thousands, are mostly of very great age, and have been used century after century to adorn the State Crowns of successive Kings and Queens.

The State Crown now in the Tower was made for Queen Victoria, in 1839, and with some alterations and additions has been so preserved by Edward VII and George V. Of the large jewels in it, such as the Black Prince's ruby, Queen Elizabeth's pearl earrings, the Stuart sapphire, the sapphire of Edward the Confessor, and the Star of South Africa,[1] historical records proclaim their origin. But the thousands of smaller stones carry with them their own age, for certain forms of cutting pertain to certain centuries. Thus the table-cut diamond is an older stone than the rose-cut, and the rose-cut is older than the brilliant. Inversely no brilliant in the present Crown could have been in that of Charles II, for this process of cutting was then unknown.

The State Crown is of the Imperial, as distinguished from the Royal shape of the older crown; thus the arches are not depressed where they cross each other, but slope up to the monde. In the band the two great stones are the Star of South Africa in front, and the Stuart sapphire exactly opposite it at the back. Between these, round the band at intervals are very large sapphires, rubies, and emeralds thickly encrusted with diamonds. Above the band

[1] See Chapter X.

are alternate crosses patés and fleurs-de-lis in diamonds, in the centre of each being a large coloured gem. Indeed, the whole Crown is a complete mass of diamonds interspersed with coloured gems and pearls. Up the arches which spring from the crosses patés are clusters of diamonds formed to represent oak leaves with the acorns represented by large pearls. The device on the arches is commemorative of the oak of Boscobel, in which Charles II hid for his life when a fugitive. The Black Prince's ruby, which is as large as an egg, is set at the foot of the front arch. The monde is covered with a complete mass of diamonds so closely set as to leave no metal visible. On top of the monde is a large cross paté, also an entire mass of diamonds, and in the centre of it is set the magnificent sapphire which was once in the coronation ring of Edward the Confessor. Where the two arches cross may be seen pendent four very large pearls as large as small birds' eggs. These were Queen Elizabeth's earrings. Inside this Crown is a purple velvet Cap of Maintenance edged round the bottom with minever. This Crown weighs 39 oz. 5 dwts.

The third Crown of the King is the Imperial Crown of India, made for George V when he was crowned Emperor of India in 1912. As mentioned elsewhere, the Crown of England is not allowed by ancient law to leave the shores of the British Isles; consequently this new Crown had to be made.

THE IMPERIAL INDIAN CROWN

The work was entrusted to the Court Jewellers, Messrs. Garrard, and a very fine example of the jeweller's art was the result. The Crown cost £60,000, and is adorned with some six thousand precious stones. These are mostly diamonds, but some very large and valuable coloured stones are also displayed. Notably a large cabuchon emerald in front of the band of the Crown, a very fine ruby in the front cross paté, and a very valuable emerald in the cross paté on top of the Crown. In shape the Crown approaches nearer the Imperial shape as pictorially known. Instead of two arches as in the other crowns there are eight demi arches which incline upwards to support the monde instead of being depressed to receive it. These demi arches spring from the eight crosses patés and fleurs-de-lis, which stand on the band of the Crown. The monde, as well as all the crosses patés and fleurs-de-lis, are a mass of diamonds with a large coloured gem in the centre of each. Inside the Crown is the Cap of Maintenance of purple velvet bound at the bottom with minever.

The Queen also has three crowns, or rather two crowns and a diadem. These are the crown first made for Mary of Modena, Queen of James II, a diadem made for the same Queen, and the present Queen Mary's State Crown.

Queen Mary of Modena's Crown is small in size, and was made to be worn on top of the head and not to fit it. The general effect may be noticed on the

statue of Queen Anne which stands outside St.
Paul's Cathedral. Indeed, this is very probably
a representation of identically this same crown. It
is adorned entirely with diamonds and pearls, and
has no coloured stones. Round the band is a con-
tinuous succession of large-sized diamonds, and
above these is a string of pearls each as large as a
pea running completely round the circumference.
Above the band alternately are crosses patés and
fleurs-de-lis, also in diamonds. From the crosses
patés spring the two arches of the crown; these are
adorned with rows of large pearls with diamonds
on each side of the rows. At the point of crossing
the arches are depressed, and on this depression
rests the monde, a mass of small diamonds. On
the monde is fixed a cross of diamonds with large
pearls at the points. The Cap is of crimson velvet
bordered at the bottom with minever.

The diadem belonging to the same Queen, and
said to have been given her by James II at a cost
of £110,000, is of a beautiful and simple design. Not
being a crown, it has no arches, and is in fact simply
a broad gold circlet thickly encrusted with diamonds,
the top edge being bordered by a row of large pearls
touching each other all the way round. In front this
row of pearls is slightly arched, and a large diamond
is fixed in the apex. The diadem is fitted with a
cap of crimson velvet bound at the bottom with
minever. This diadem was worn by Mary of Modena

DIADEM OF QUEEN MARY OF MODENA,
WIFE OF JAMES II

THE QUEEN'S STATE CROWN.

Reproduced by permission of Messrs. Cassell & Co., from a painting made by Mr. Cyril Davenport (Copyright).

on the way to her Coronation, and during the
ceremony it was replaced by the Crown, above
described, which she wore as she returned to the
Palace in State with the King.

The most important and most beautiful of the
Queen's crowns is that which belongs to Her present
Majesty, for not only is it officially, but privately
the property of Queen Mary, though three of the
great diamonds in it may belong to the State. It
was designed and made by Messrs. Garrard, and is
certainly of great credit to twentieth century workmanship. The crown is set with diamonds throughout, no coloured stones having been used. In front
of the band is one of the four large Stars of Africa,
and round the band are alternate roses and crosses
composed of diamonds. The rims of the band are
also set continuously with small diamonds. On the
band stand three fleurs-de-lis and three crosses patés
alternately, all set with diamonds. In the centre of
the front cross paté is the great and historic Koh-i-
Nur diamond.[1] From the fleurs-de-lis and crosses
paté spring six demi arches which slope gracefully
upwards to support the monde. The monde is
completely encrusted with small diamonds. On
the monde stands a cross paté, in the centre of which
is displayed another of the Stars of Africa, drop-
shaped with the point downwards. Inside the
Crown is a purple velvet cap lined at the bottom

[1] See p. 151.

with minever. The Crown is of considerable size, made to fit the head instead of standing on it, as does the older Crown of Queen Mary of Modena.

The Prince of Wales' Crown, as it is called, but more correctly the Crown of the eldest son of the King, is at the Tower. This is distinct from Prince of Wales' Coronet, which is kept at Carnarvon Castle. It is the King's prerogative to make whom he pleases Prince of Wales, but usually, as at present, the title is given to the eldest son. The Crown at the Tower is very simple and only differs in general appearance from the coronets of some members of the peerage in having one arch over it, supporting a gold monde and cross. Above the band stand alternately four gold fleurs-de-lis and four gold crosses patés. Inside is a crimson velvet cap edged at the bottom with minever. The eldest son of the King places this Crown on his own head during the Coronation service at the same time as the peers put on their coronets. On later occasions it is placed on a stool before the Prince when he attends at the House of Lords when the King opens Parliament in State.

The Coronet of the Prince of Wales, as such, which as mentioned is kept at Carnarvon, is a more beautiful and graceful insignia. It consists of a circlet of gold adorned with pearls and amethysts. Above the circlet stand alternately four crosses patés and four fleurs-de-lis. These all are pierced

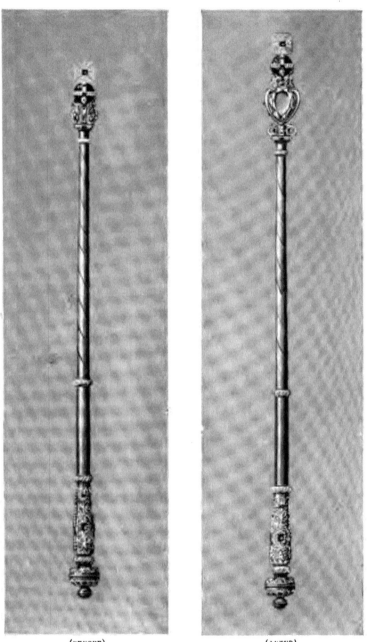

(BEFORE)   (AFTER)
THE KING'S ROYAL SCEPTRE BEFORE AND AFTER THE INTRODUCTION
OF THE STAR OF AFRICA

and within the outlines of the former are sprays of the Rose of England and of the latter the Daffodil of Wales. The daffodil with a certain amount of excusable heraldic elasticity, is introduced in place of the more homely though less picturesque leek, the hitherto best known emblem of the Little Sister. Between the crosses patés and the fleurs-de-lis are rosebud sprays. This Coronet was made throughout of Welsh gold, by Messrs. Garrard, in 1911, for Edward, the present Prince of Wales.

THE SCEPTRES

Next to the crowns in emblematic importance and kingly dignity come the sceptres. Of these there are in all five in the Jewel House, each with its special history and significance. The greatest and most important of these is the King's Royal Sceptre with the Cross. It is of gold, richly jewelled, about three feet long, and was made for Charles II, remaining practically the same till the reign of Edward VII. When the Stars of Africa[1] were presented to that monarch he decided to have the largest portion placed in the head of the Sceptre, but explicit orders were given that no part of the old Sceptre was to be removed, the diamond was merely to be inserted. This proved a very difficult problem, but was successfully solved by Messrs. Garrard, as a comparison of drawings of the Sceptre

[1] See p. 162.

before and after clearly show. As seen now, the Star of Africa is the central attraction, not only from its huge size, but its extraordinary brilliancy. It is drop-shaped, 2⅜ in. in length and 1⅛ in. in width, and weighs 516½ carats. It is held in place by four very ingeniously contrived gold clasps, which can be opened and the diamond taken out when required to be worn as a pendant. Above the diamond on enamelled scrolls stands the great amethyst orb which is faceted all over, and has round the centre a jewelled band with an arch of gold, rubies, and diamonds. On top of the amethyst orb is fixed the Cross, made entirely of diamonds with a large emerald in the centre. These all form the head of the Sceptre.

Below the great diamond the fleur-de-lis of the old Sceptre has been cleverly depressed into the form of a support; this is thickly jewelled with coloured gems and diamonds, and below this again is a jewelled band. Near the hilt of the Sceptre is a smooth portion for the grip ; above this is a collar of gems and enamels, and below another similar collar having rich sprays of gold and enamels, thickly jewelled with coloured stones and diamonds. At the butt is a sphere encrusted with enamels and precious stones. When the King holds this Sceptre, he may veritably be said to have in his hand a King's ransom.

The King's Sceptre with the Dove comes next in

importance. It is a rod of gold three feet seven inches in length. At the top is a monde or orb of gold with a fillet round the centre studded with diamonds, and with an arch above similarly jewelled. From the top of the monde rises a golden cross, on which is sitting a white enamelled dove with extended wings, its eyes, beak, and feet of gold. Below the monde is a band studded with diamonds, and beneath this another band with drooping designs, ornamented with coloured gems and diamonds. In the centre of the Sceptre is an ornamental band of enamels and gems, and gold open-work with coloured gems, enamels, and diamonds. Nearer to the bottom of the Sceptre is another band with large jewels. The boss at the foot of the Sceptre is encircled by two bands, one jewelled and the other enamelled. The Dove is symbolical of the Holy Ghost. This Sceptre is borne in the sovereign's left hand during one portion of the ceremony at the Coronation.

Next we have the Queen's Sceptre with the Cross which was originally made for Queen Mary of Modena. It is made of gold ornamented with diamonds, and is two feet ten inches in length. At the top is a double fleur-de-lis thickly set with fair-sized diamonds. Above this is a golden monde, round which is a fillet thickly adorned with diamonds, the arch over the monde being similarly decorated. On the monde stands a cross which has a large dia-mond on each of its arms and one in the centre. The middle of the Sceptre is ornamented with sprays formed of open-work in gold, with leaves and flowers composed of large and small diamonds. The Sceptre ends with an elaborately jewelled boss.

The Queen's Sceptre with the Dove resembles that of the King, but is rather smaller and is differently ornamented. Thus the fillet encircling the monde and the arch over it are ornamented with coloured gems as well as diamonds, and with leaves enamelled red and white. At the middle of the Sceptre is a collar of dark blue enamel, ornamented with gems and designs in white enamel. Near the foot is another more elaborate collar with sprays of open-work in gold, ornamented thickly with gems and enamels. At the foot is a boss with ornaments of gold, gems, and enamels. This sceptre was lost for many years, but was eventually found, in 1814, hidden at the back of a shelf in the Jewel House.

The Queen's Ivory Rod was destroyed by the Commonwealth, but a replica of it was made for Queen Mary of Modena, and this is now in the Jewel House. This Rod or Sceptre also has a dove on top of it, but with closed wings. It stands on a gold cross which in its turn rises from a gold monde. The dove has golden eyes, beak, and feet. The Rod, which, as its name implies, is made of ivory, is in three pieces, with collars of gold at the joining points. Its total length is three feet one and a half inches. The boss at the bottom is very similar to

The King's Sceptre
before the
Star of Africa
was introduced.

The Queen's Sceptre
with the Cross.

THE KING'S ORB.

Reproduced by permission of Messrs. Cassell & Co., from a painting made by Mr. Cyril Davenport (*Copyright*).

the monde at the top, and both are ornamented with champlevé enamels.

St. Edward's Staff, known also from very early days as the Rod of Justice and Equity, is a replica made for Charles II of the ancient staff destroyed by the Commonwealth. It is much longer than any of the sceptres, being four feet seven and a half inches in length, and being intended to be used as a walking staff, is shod with a spike of steel like an alpine-stock. It is made of plain bright gold, and at the top has a gold monde surmounted by a gold cross. In the monde of the original Staff was a piece of the true cross. This Staff is emblematically intended to guide the King's footsteps in the way he should go.

THE ORBS

There are two Orbs in the Jewel House, one for the King and the other for the Queen. The orb is a very ancient Christian emblem, and signifies the domination of the Christian religion over the world. It may be described as a globe of gold on which stands a cross. The King's Orb, which is known as the Orb of England, is a very valuable and richly gemmed emblem, and is only placed in the hand of the King or Queen who is actual sovereign of the realm. The Queen's Orb, which is of somewhat less importance and value, and smaller in size, is the insignia of a Queen Consort.

The King's Orb is a golden globe six inches in

diameter, round the centre of which is a fillet of
gold outlined with fine pearls and ornamented with
clusters of gems, the gems being set in borders of
white and red enamel. The centre stones of these
clusters are large rubies, sapphires, and emeralds,
each surrounded by diamonds. Over the top of the
Orb is an arch of similar design and similarly
jewelled. Standing on the Orb is a large amethyst
on which is fixed the cross. The amethyst is of
remarkable size and beauty, one and a half inches
in height and faceted all over. The cross is a very
beautiful one, and has in the centre on one side an
emerald and on the other a sapphire, each surrounded
with diamonds. The outlines of the cross are marked
by rows of diamonds, and there are three large
diamonds along the centre of each arm. At the foot
of the cross, where it rests on the great amethyst,
is a collar of diamonds. At the ends of each of the
arms is a large pearl, and in each of the four inner
corners is also a large pearl. This Orb was made for
Charles II by Sir Robert Vyner to replace an older
orb destroyed by the Commonwealth.

The Queen's Orb owes its origin to Mary, wife of
William of Orange. By right of succession, Mary
was Queen of England, and William her Consort,
but she insisted on a joint occupation of the throne.
Thus it came about that William III was crowned
King of England and took the King's Orb in his
hand, whilst a smaller replica was made for Queen

Mary. Though in general appearance they are much alike, the Queen's Orb is not so important or handsome as that of the King. The globe is of polished gold, and round it is a fillet outlined with large pearls and studded with rubies, sapphires, and emeralds. These coloured stones are alternately circular and octagonal, and are set in collars of gold. The arch over the Orb is ornamented in a similar manner. The cross, which stands on top, is studded with rubies, sapphires, and diamonds, differently arranged on either side.

D

CHAPTER III

THE REGALIA—*continued*

The Jewelled State Sword—The most valuable in the world—
The emerald worth £2700—The sword described—The King offers
it to the Church and redeems it for 100 shillings—The sword
lost and found—The Sword of State—Carried before the King—
The sword described—The three swords of Henry VIII—
" Defender of the Faith"—The Sword Spiritual—The Sword
Temporal—" Curtana," or the Sword of Mercy—St. George's
golden spurs—The Bracelets—Bracelets worn by King Saul as
well as Babylonian and Assyrian monarchs—The Coronation
rings—The King's ring—The Queen's ring—Queen Victoria's
ring—Charles II's Coronation ring—Coronation ring of Edward
the Confessor—James II's monde—Model of the Koh-i-Nur
—Model of the Cullinan Diamond—Chisel and hammer.

THE Jewelled State Sword is the most beautiful and valuable sword in the world. To illustrate its value it may be mentioned that one stone alone, a square emerald set at cross of the hilt, is worth at least £2700, and this is only one of scores of precious stones which adorn this Sword. The grip is one mass of diamonds, which give so brilliant an effect that the beautiful designs are almost lost to sight; these are, however, when looked closely into, oak leaves and acorns. These may be, as in the State Crown, emblematic of Charles II and his oak tree,

though perhaps, and more prophetically, an emblem
of old England : the mighty oak that built her
ships, and through them made her what she is in
this year of grace.

At the head of the hilt of the Sword is a large
and very valuable diamond, which has on its four
sides four large rubies, and below these two rows
of large emeralds and diamonds. The " quillions,"
as the cross-piece between the hilt and the blade
is called, is encrusted with a mass of small diamonds,
so thickly set that the gold beneath is scarcely
visible. At the extremities of the quillions are
lions' heads beautifully modelled and also formed
entirely of small diamonds set close together.

The blade of the Sword is of Damascus steel of
the very finest temper, and is in itself of great
value. The scabbard is of dull gold ornamented
throughout its length with jewels, both large and
small. At the upper end is a cross formed of a
sapphire, a ruby, two diamonds, and a yellow
sapphire ; this latter a rare and valuable stone·
This rich cross is enclosed with laurel sprays of
diamonds. Looking down the scabbard we see
first the Rose of England, portrayed by a ruby
set thickly round with diamonds. Then comes the
Thistle of Scotland, fashioned out of rubies,
emeralds, and diamonds ; and next the Shamrock
of Ireland, appropriately formed of emeralds alone.
These three devices are thrice repeated as the

scabbard fines away to a point. Between the devices are crossed golden sprays of laurel and palm leaves. On the " chape " or butt end of the scabbard appear again oak leaves and acorns formed of small diamonds. At the extreme tip is a large and very beautiful turquoise, oblong in shape, and set around with diamonds.

Naturally a sword of this magnificence is meant more for display on State occasions than for use on the field of battle; indeed, from a swordsman's point of view, it would be quite impossible to firmly grip a hilt made of diamonds and other angularly cut stones. The scabbard and jewels are not ancient, whatever the history of the blade may be, having been made for the Coronation of George IV, just one hundred years ago. Since that reign this has been the Sword which the King at his Coronation hands to the Archbishop of Canterbury as symbolising that he places his Sword at the service of the Church. Happily for the financial stability of the empire, it is arranged between Church and State that after each Coronation the Keeper of the Jewel House is empowered to redeem the said Sword by paying to the Archbishop the apparently in-adequate recompense of 100 shillings.

The Sword was rarely used except at coronations, and not being carefully guarded as it now is, got lost or mislaid in the reign of Queen Victoria, possibly because a queen has no use for a sword. For some

decades this priceless weapon disappeared entirely,
and then was only accidentally found at the back
of an old disused cupboard. How truly British,
both friends and semi-friends, will alike exclaim !
Doubtless numbers of people had seen the box
containing it, but as this box closely resembles an
ordinary gun case, it was probably taken for one
and left undisturbed. In this box, which looks like
a gun case, are the emplacements for two swords.
One is for the Jewelled Sword, but what lay in the
other is not recorded—possibly a less ornate weapon
for the King's ordinary use when in uniform. This
latter has disappeared probably amongst the cast-off
accoutrements of some bygone monarch.

The Sword of State which is carried before the
King at the opening of Parliament is quite a different
weapon. It is a long, two-handed sword, with a
gold hilt and quillion, and is encased in a crimson
velvet scabbard. The length of the blade alone is
32 in., and the breadth of the same about 2 in.
This is the Sword with which the King knighted
the Prince of Wales when he was created a Knight
of the Garter. The quillion of the sword is formed
of an elongated lion on one side, and a similarly
maltreated unicorn on the other. On the hilt are
raised representations of a portcullis, a fleur-de-lis,
and a harp. On the pommel are a thistle, an orb,
and other emblems. Down the scabbard are various
designs in gold, such as portcullis, the lion standing

on a crown, orb, and cross. Then more conspicuously the Royal arms of England, the double Tudor rose, the thistle of Scotland, the harp of Ireland, and the fleur-de-lis of France.

The remaining three swords in the Jewel House are of a set, and were sent to Henry VIII by the Pope as Defender of the Faith. Henry VIII, as we know, disagreed with the Pope over his first matrimonial venture, and throwing His Holiness overboard, so to speak, made himself sole head of the Church of England. This bold deed, though based on a personal matter, was the foundation of England's greatness. The swords the King retained, as also the title, which is still born by English sovereigns, and appears on their coins to this day: "Georgius V. D.G. Britt: Omn: Rex. F.D. Ind. Imp:". These three swords are named the Sword Spiritual, the Sword Temporal, and "Curtana," or the Sword of Mercy. They are long, straight swords with broad blades of exactly similar pattern, but there is one curious difference between Curtana and the other two, for the blade of this sword has had about six inches of blade broken off, leaving a blunt point. This break and shortening are intended to portray the element of Mercy.

The Golden Spurs, known as St. George's Spurs, which are one of the King's military emblems now to be seen in the Tower, were made for Charles II by Sir Robert Vyner, and were copied from the pair that existed in former ages, and which were sold or melted down by the Commonwealth. They are of the pattern known as "prick" spurs, for instead of rowels they have one sharp point. The straps are of crimson velvet embroidered in gold.

Bracelets have long been a regal emblem, being old even when Saul, King of Israel, was slain and the Amalekite brought his crown and bracelet to King David. The Babylonian and Assyrian monarchs wore bracelets as one of the insignia of royalty, whilst at the present day the Shah is the only male person in Persia who has a right to wear a bracelet. What may be the exact significance of the bracelet is not clear ; it may have none, and may in the course of ages have become by usage one of the insignia of a reigning monarch. The bracelets at present in the Jewel House were made by Sir Robert Vyner for Charles II from some ancient design, and are of solid gold. On them are enamelled designs representing the emblems of the three kingdoms, as well as the fleur-de-lis of France. They are lined with crimson velvet.

A recent addition to the Crown Jewels in the Tower are the Coronation Rings. These are the private property of their Majesties, who with their usual gracious forethought have sent them to the Tower so that all their subjects may see them. The Coronation Rings are three in number : the King's Ring, the Queen's Ring, and a special ring made for Queen Victoria and presented to her by her uncle, William IV.

The King's Ring is not ancient, dating only to the reign of William IV, and is of a magnificence that makes it unsuitable for daily wear even by a king in these days. In the centre is a very large and valuable sapphire which could not now be bought for £1000. Lying over this, in the form of a cross, are four long, narrow rubies. Round the whole is a circle of diamonds. The general design is to represent the Cross of St. George on a blue shield, as it is in insignia of the Order of the Garter.

The Queen's Ring is not so large or ambitious, and might be worn without being unduly pronounced on ordinary occasions. In the centre is a large rectangular ruby set around with diamonds. The ruby is one of remarkable beauty and considerable value.

The third ring at the Jewel House is a small replica of the King's Ring, and was bequeathed by William IV to the then Heir-Apparent to the throne, the Princess Victoria. A kindly thought on the part of the old King, knowing that a very large man's ring would not be suitable for a young girl-queen. Unfortunately the jeweller was too much of a courtier, and made the ring so small that it caused Queen Victoria intense agony. The sapphire in this ring, though smaller, is so perfect as to be in value equal to the larger stone in the King's Ring.

A much older Coronation ring than any of these is probably in existence. It belonged to Charles II, and was amongst the Stuart relics bequeathed to George III by Cardinal York. Where it is, or who owns it, is not known, for it must be remembered that these Coronation rings are the private property of each Sovereign and are at their disposal. It was therefore open to George III to give or bequeath it to whom he pleased.

Older far than any of these is the sapphire now in the cross paté on the summit of the King's State Crown, which was in the Coronation ring of Edward the Confessor nearly 900 years ago. Perchance some future King will transpose the two sapphires as a matter of sentiment, replacing Edward the Confessor's sapphire in the Coronation ring and transferring the sapphire now in that ring to the · cross paté.

A typical example of the depredations to which the Crown Jewels were subject in less guarded days is shown in the Jewel House. This is a jewel which passed for long as a magnificent faceted aquamarine, in the shape of a monde or globe surmounted by a diamond cross, which figured first on top of the Crown of King James II. Many historians mention this stone with speechless admiration. Yet when a more critical age came to examine this precious

stone, it was found to be nothing more valuable
than a ball of coloured glass! Naturally when
this discovery was made the ornament lost its
place of honour on top of the King's Crown, and is
now shown only as a curiosity. Whether the
original aquamarine had been disposed of by
James II before his flight or sold in some long
past reign by order of the King, or whether owing
to slack guardianship it was removed through the
connivance of the guardians and replaced by a
worthless imitation, history does not relate. At
any rate, an expert goldsmith and jeweller must
have been in the secret for the making of an exact
replica, and must have required prolonged possession
of the model to work from. Probably, too, when
the substitution was first discovered nobody cared
to say much about it lest they themselves should be
suspected of theft, or at least accused of criminal
carelessness in its custody.

Amongst the Jewels may be seen a model of the
Koh-i-Nur diamond as it was before being cut into
the form of a brilliant. It was at that period set in
an armlet with two lesser diamonds on either side,
and could either thus be worn, or alternatively as an
ornament in the turban, by the Eastern potentate
who then owned the great diamond. This model is
set in the original setting of gold, richly enamelled.
The crimson silk cords ending in tassels of pearls
and rubies, with which the armlet was furnished,

are also shown in original. This model shows the curious conical shape the diamond then had from which its name, "The Mountain of Light," was derived. A looking-glass set behind it enables one to see the beautiful enamels at the back of the setting.

Another model of great interest is that of the Cullinan diamond or the Star of Africa, exactly showing its size and appearance when first found. It is difficult to imagine a diamond of this size and appearance until we actually see the model. It will be found described amongst the greater gems in another place.

The Star of Africa was, it will be remembered, cut into four great portions, whilst numerous small pieces also resulted. This operation was performed at Amsterdam by the famous diamond-cutters, Messrs. Coster. The hammer and chisel with which this delicate operation was performed are kept in the Jewel House, and are most unlikely-looking instruments. The chisel is in the shape of a deep man's comb without a handle, and is more like a wedge than a chisel, as generally understood. It is of hardened steel, yet not so hard but that it shows the marks where it struck the diamond. The hammer is equally unconventional, being a solid steel cylinder, like a short rod or truncheon. Apparently only three or four sharp blows opposite the natural cleavages were sufficient to break up the great rough stone into the four great Stars of Africa.

It is difficult by word of mouth, or with the pen, or even by illustrations, to give an adequate idea of the splendour and brilliancy of the Crown Jewels. They have to be seen to be adequately appreciated. This by the gracious permission of His Majesty the King it is possible for all, rich or poor, to achieve by visiting the Jewel House at the Tower of London. The poor can see them without toll or fee on what are known as "free days," whilst the rich need only spend sixpence for the same privilege on "paying days." If these chapters in any way help to give an added interest to their visit they will have amply achieved their object.

CHAPTER IV

THE ROYAL PLATE

Plate for the Royal table—Plate for the King's Chapel—Trumpets and maces—Queen Elizabeth's gold salt cellar—Escapes the Commonwealth—The design of the salt cellar—The State salt of Charles II—Presented by the City of Exeter—A jewelled castle armed with golden guns—Charles II's wine fountain— Presented by the Borough of Plymouth—The finest specimen of plate in the Jewel House—Not only ornamental, but useful to His Majesty—The ordeal of the lady on top—The eleven St. George's Salts—Curious history of a set of four—A correspondence that lasted ninety-two years—The ordeal of the serpents— St. George on the canopy of the great salts—The salt spoons— Two golden tankards—To be viewed from a discreet distance— The silver trumpets—Used at Coronations—And when Peace is Proclaimed—Crimson and gold bannerets—The Archbishop's old time exhortation—The maces of the sergeants-at-arms—Charles II, James II, William and Mary, George I—The mace originally a bludgeon—The crown at head of it the insignia of Royal authority —The policeman's truncheon a miniature mace—The maces at the Proclamation of Peace—The mace-bearers originally a corps of knights—Bodyguard of the King.

THE Royal Plate in the Jewel House may be roughly divided into two main categories, the one being plate for the Royal table and dignity, and the other ecclesiastical plate for use at Coronations or at services in one of His Majesty's Chapels Royal. The table

plate consists mostly of large gold salt cellars,
know Salts of State, whilst the kingly dignity
is represented great gold maces borne by
the sergeants-at-arms, which sound a fanfare when the king silver trumpets

The oldest piece of table plate in the Jewel H.
is Queen Elizabeth's gold salt cellar. How this
escaped the depredations of the Commonwealth, or
how it avoided being melted down with other
Royal plate, to meet the necessities of Charles I,
history does not relate. Very possibly it was
sold in those days, and preserved by the purchaser through the troublous times, and then
either given back, or sold back, to the Crown on
the Restoration.

The salt cellar, which is a very fine specimen of
Elizabethan work, stands about a foot in height;
at the top is a shallow pan in which the salt was
placed, over which is a gold canopy supported on
brackets. The object of canopies such as this
apparently was to keep the larger and more obtrusive pieces of dirt and dust from the rough rafters
overhead, from falling into the salt. Salt was a
precious thing in those days, and as carefully to be
protected as would *pâté de foie gras* in these times.
On top of the canopy stands a knight in armour
holding a long two-handed sword and a shield.
He also is manifestly guarding the salt from theft
and danger.

With the exception of this one piece, none of the gold table plate in the Jewel House dates further back than the reign of Charles II, and this for good and sufficient reasons, as we have seen. To renew the Royal Plate at the Restoration several contributions were made, and the chiefest of these by the loyal county of Devon. The city of Exeter presented His Majesty with a magnificent golden State salt cellar, fashioned like a castle ; and the Borough of Plymouth came forward with one of the handsomest pieces of gold plate in existence, a beautiful wine fountain.

The State salt cellar stands nearly two feet high, and is a most elaborate and beautifully worked out representation of a square castle prepared for defence as it would be in medieval days. At each corner are turrets for flank defence, and cannons and guns bristle from every wall. On the top is a cupolo shaped like a Royal crown, and under this may be seen exquisitely fashioned field-guns on wheels. The castle is adorned throughout with precious stones, one specially large sapphire being observable above the portcullis at the front entrance. Some historians think it was intended to represent the White Tower, which is the keep of the Tower of London, but as many castles in those days were more or less of this design, and amongst them Exeter Castle, it seems more probable that the design was taken from that city.

The tops of the four turrets as well as the crown left off and disclosed shallow pans or saucers each capable of holding a small quantity of precious salt. There are also small troughs under the windows also intended each to hold a little salt. Probably nobody but the King and Queen and three or four distinguished guests seated near were intended to take salt from the State salt cellar, its place being in the centre of the great banqueting table exactly opposite the King.

The wine fountain, besides being an exceedingly fine example of the goldsmith's art, must have been a very acceptable and appropriate present for the jovial King to receive. The fountain stands two and a half feet high, the central figure being a lady very lightly clad, holding a snake by the neck. Below the lady are two tiers of shallow receptacles shaped like shells and ornamented with mermaids, dolphins, and sea nymphs. The lower, and larger tier, measures 28 in. in diameter. When in use the fountain could be made to play as does a water-fountain in the garden. The procedure would be to place a barrel of wine in the gallery : from this a pipe would run which could be fixed to the hollow at the base of the fountain. When the tap was turned on the wine would run up inside the lady and out presumedly through the serpent's mouth. The height of spray would depend on the height of the barrel above the table. The wine as it fell in spray would drip down the lady, which impending deluge doubtless accounts for her lack of garments; thence it would flow into the tier of smaller receptacles. As these filled up they would overflow into the larger receptacles below, and when these in their turn were filled to overflowing, the only way to prevent a flood, and a devastating waste of good wine, was for the company to continuously dip their beakers into them and thus stem the tide by steadily drinking the contents.

There are eleven other great gold salt cellars amongst the Royal plate at the Tower dating from the reign of Charles II, which used to help in decorating the tables at Coronation banquets. These are all known as St. George's Salts and are of several patterns.

A curious story attaches to one set of four of these salt cellars. They are cylindrical in shape, rather like a deep drum, and embossed with sprays of leaves and flowers in high relief. At the top are three brackets curving outwards fashioned as serpents. When the Royal plate was being overhauled for the Coronation of George IV, some bright expert decided that the brackets were not brackets, but legs, and turned the salts over and stood them on these. He was then faced by an aching void which would hold a couple of pounds of salt, for the cylinders are hollow. Naught dismayed, he had shallow gold pans to hold salt made to fit the cylinders,

E

and on these were engraved the Royal arms and the
words " George IV." Thus upside down the salts
remained for ninety-two years, the serpents standing
on their heads, and the herbaceous ornamentation
drooping sadly. During those ninety-two years an
animated correspondence appears to have been
carried on as to which end upwards the salts should
rightly stand, and it was only in the time of the
present Keeper of the Jewel House that the serpents,
doubtless to their relief, were allowed again to hold
up their heads, and the golden flowers and foliage
were condemned no longer to droop. The real
mission in life of these brackets, as has been re-
discovered in this post-bellum age, is to support
a napkin which was spread over them so as to protect
the salt from dust and dirt.

All the rest of the St. George's Salts have a permanent golden canopy over them very similar to that
which covers Queen Elizabeth's salt cellar. On top
of the canopy in each case is a knight in armour,
in some cases mounted, in others on foot. The
knight is probably meant for St. George, in some
cases mounted before killing the dragon, and in
others dismounted and at rest, after having accomplished that historic feat.

Appertaining to the great salt cellars there
remain a residue of twelve gold salt spoons, the
missing numbers no doubt having been lost, or
annexed by excessively loyal guests.

Two very handsome gold tankards are in the Jewel House, which were added to the Royal plate by George IV. Viewed from a discreet distance the effect is very fine, but a closer inspection is not recommended to those who disapprove of realism in art. Queen Victoria, it is reported, disliked these flagons intensely.

The silver trumpets and gold maces are placed in the Jewel House as part of the Royal Treasure. There were originally sixteen silver trumpets, but one disappeared in a bygone reign and has never been recovered, so that fifteen only remain. They are the ordinary shape of a cavalry trumpet, and are used not only at the King's Coronation, but also when proclamations are made by the Heralds in the King's name. They were thus used, for instance, when the Heralds rode to various parts of London and proclaimed the Peace at the end of the Great War, in 1919. Pendent from each trumpet is a crimson silk banneret richly embroidered in gold, displaying the Royal arms with the cypher of the reigning monarch. At the Coronation of the sovereign the trumpeters blow a fanfare on these silver trumpets, the ritual for which in the old world wording of the Coronation service is thus given :

" The Archbishop of Canterbury speaks thus to the people : ' Sirs, I here present unto you King George, the undoubted King of this realm : wherefore all you who are come this day to do your homage, are you willing to do the same?' The people signify their willingness by loud and repeated exclamations, all with one voice crying out 'God save King George.'"

Then the trumpets sound a fanfare.

Of gold maces there are eight in number at the Tower. The oldest of these are two made for Charles II; there are two also which date from the reign of James II, whilst three were supplied for William and Mary, and one for George I. They are all of very similar pattern. A mace was originally a weapon used by cavalry soldiers, and many and various patterns of these may be seen in the Armoury in the White Tower. It was, in fact, a bludgeon with a short handle and a heavy head, sufficiently heavy to beat in the steel helmets worn in those days. The ceremonial mace has, instead of a battle-head, a crown, and this crown is to denote the delegation of the Royal authority. The Sergeant-at-arms carrying the mace before the Speaker, and placing it on rests before him in the House of Commons, thus conveys the Royal Assent to the assembly. In the same way mayors of towns have crowned maces borne before with the same intention. When policemen, or peelers as they were then called, were first incorporated, they were served out with truncheons which were miniature maces with a Royal crown at the head of each. These crowns, however, were not very practical weapons with which to knock a burglar on the head; indeed, they generally broke off, which was an untoward catastrophe, so they were discontinued. Those who were in the streets of London when the Peace proclamation was made at the close of the Great War, will have noticed that sergeants-at-arms bearing their maces accompanied the heralds and trumpeters, thus signifying that the whole ceremony was with the King's authority.

At the coronation of a sovereign the sergeants-at-arms, whose number seems to have varied in the course of centuries, carry their maces and form part of the procession. Originally the mace-bearers were a corps of twenty-four knights, or gentlemen of high degree, who formed a sort of bodyguard to the King, and thus they were in the reign of Richard Cœur de Lion. As late as the reign of Charles II the sergeants-at-arms bearing their maces are shown mounted on horses. At the present day a sergeant-at-arms walks and carries his mace, no mean weight, as those who have seen them stagger after a long day may well imagine. Thirty-four pounds do they each weigh.

We have now accounted for all the secular plate in the Tower pertaining to royalty, and proceed to describe the ecclesiastical plate used at the coronations of our monarchs, or on certain occasions during their reigns, either at Westminster, or at St. Peter ad Vincula, a Royal chapel within the Tower.

CHAPTER V

ECCLESIASTICAL PLATE

The Ampulla or Golden Eagle—It's great age—Repaired for Coronation of Charles II—The lapis lazuli eagle lost or sold—The
Ampulla escapes the Commonwealth—Hidden in Westminster
Abbey—The Ampulla at the Coronation—Filled with holy
oil—Oil costing £200—Height of eagle—A prototype of the
lecternes in churches—The anointing spoon—Of Byzantine
origin—The spoon described—Its use at a coronation—Oil on
the King's head—The Maundy Dish—Its severe simplicity—
Inaugurated by Charles II—Maundy money for the aged poor—
The ceremony of presentation at Westminster—The baptismal
font—For Princes and Princesses of the Blood Royal—The
alms dish—Queen Victoria orders a new font—The bacchanalian flagons—The alms dish and flagon of William and Mary—
Used in the chapel within the Tower.

THE ecclesiastical plate, if so it may be
called, which is kept at the Tower, apper-
tains to religious ceremonies, chiefly in
connection with coronation of the sovereigns called upon to reign over the British Empire
and the baptism of the Royal children. But also
there are pieces of church plate which are used on
certain set occasions, as is in due course set forth.
The oldest piece of plate, ecclesiastical or secular,
preserved in the Tower, is the Ampulla or Golden

Eagle. This bears distinct traces of Byzantine origin, and thus may be fourteen hundred years old. It was for long attributed to Sir Robert Vyner, and was supposed to have been made for the Coronation of Charles II. But recent exact examination by experts has shown that the eagle is of a very much earlier origin. To one skilled in such matters it is, for instance, at once apparent that the screw with which the head is attached to the body is of a pattern that was ancient even in the days of Charles II, and further a close examination of the body of the eagle shows distinct signs of Byzantine workmanship.[1] It may thus be concluded that this eagle was used in very early days for the Coronation of English Kings. It then was supplanted perhaps for centuries by a much more ornate and intrinsically valuable emblem of lapis lazuli, with a golden eagle at the top enriched with pearls and diamonds, mentioned by Mezeray. This valuable bird has disappeared altogether, and whether it was disposed of to meet the necessities of Charles I, or whether sold or destroyed by the Commonwealth, is not clear. But the older eagle survived these troublous times owing to the fortunate circumstance that it was hidden and forgotten in the Treasure House at Westminster Abbey. Much mutilated, and with the wings broken off, it was handed over to Sir Robert Vyner, who restored it for the Coronation

[1] *The Crown Jewels of England*, by Younghusband and Davenport, p. 34.

of Charles II to the form in which we see it at present in the Tower.

The eagle, far from being of life size, is only nine inches high, and is in truth a very poor representation of an eagle, thus further emphasizing its ancient origin. It is, however, of solid gold hollowed only sufficiently to contain a small quantity of holy oil. This is introduced by unscrewing the head and pouring the oil into it, the holy unguent being composed chiefly of olive oil and balm. Of so great a value is it, that it is on record that James II paid no less than £200 for the small quantity required for his Coronation ceremony. The Ampulla is the prototype of the large brass eagle which we see in many churches bearing the Holy Bible on its back, emblematically about to fly to the four corners of the earth carrying the sacred message of the gospel.

At the Coronation, when the moment for the anointing of the King arrives, a small portion of the holy oil is poured into the anointing spoon, the beak of the eagle forming the channel.

The anointing spoon, into which the oil is poured from the Ampulla, can probably claim almost equally ancient origin. On this, too, recent examination has discovered distinct traces of Byzantine workmanship. So ancient a spoon has naturally been repaired and renewed from time to time during the centuries, but that it has existed for more than a thousand years is quite evident. The handle of the spoon is seven and a half inches long, tapering towards the top, showing that it is intended to be gripped with the whole hand, instead of being balanced on the fingers as are more modern spoons. It is richly ornamented and set with pearls. The bowl of the spoon is two and a quarter inches in length, and is curiously divided longitudinally by a ridge. When in use at a coronation, the Archbishop of Canterbury dips his two first fingers into the holy oil resting in these two compartments, and with the oil thus raised makes a cross on the King's head, on his breast, and on the palms of his hands. The Coronation service directs the Archbishop to pour the holy oil on to His Majesty's head, but being a kindly prelate, he does not obey these instructions · too literally, thus saving the Royal person and robes from a devastating deluge.

That this Ampulla and the spoon escaped the studied destruction of the Commonwealth is proved by the records of the Restoration, for it is expressly stated that, " All the Regalia, *except the ampulla and spoon*, both of which were constantly kept in the Church of Westminster, were sacrilegiously plundered."

One of the most impressive pieces of ecclesiastical plate, impressive from its severe simplicity, is the Maundy Dish. In contrast to the highly decorative alms dish of William and Mary, it is perfectly plain. In diameter it is somewhat over two feet, and it weighs two hundred and two ounces. It was made in the reign of Charles II in 1660–61, who decided, in place of continuing the ancient custom of distributing the Royal Bounty, to make instead an offering to the aged poor. The number of the aged poor to be thus beneficed is regulated by the King's age, that is to say, if he is fifty years of age, fifty old men and fifty old women receive the bounty. The bounty itself consists of a silver penny, a silver twopenny, a silver threepenny, and a silver fourpenny, making a total of tenpence. This in Charles II days was a fairly handsome dole ; whilst even at this day the set of four silver coins is of a value far above its intrinsic merits. Indeed, on one occasion a five pound note was given at the Abbey door for the purchase of one of these sets. In addition, however, to the coins, the aged poor who are yearly selected by the Dean of Westminster receive other handsome doles from the King in money and clothing.

The ceremony takes place in Westminster Abbey on the Thursday before Good Friday, known as Maundy Thursday. The dish is taken from the Tower to Westminster, where at the ceremony a yeoman of the guard carries it in procession, holding displayed the little red bags containing the Maundy Money. The aged poor are marshalled on each side of the aisle, and to them after an impressive service the little bags of money are one by one distributed, by the clergy, in the King's name.

It will be noticed that William and Mary have placed their cypher in the middle of the Maundy Dish, but the plate mark clearly shows that it was made at the beginning of the reign of Charles II.

After the ceremony at Westminster the Maundy Dish is conveyed back to the Tower, and there rests behind iron bars for yet another year.

Of the ecclesiastical plate the most prominent piece is the gold baptismal font made for Charles II, and intended to be used for the baptism of all Royal children born thereafter. If the original intention had been carried out a very long successions of Princes and Princesses, including those now living, would have had this historic connection with an ancient piece of church plate. Unhappily, however, owing possibly to the inadvertence of Court officials or the clergy, the font has only been spasmodically used. The first recorded occasion is at the christening of the Princess Augusta, afterwards Duchess of Brunswick, the third daughter of Frederick Louis, Prince of Wales in the year 1737. We also know that it was used at the baptism of George IV, and for the same ceremony in the case of twelve of the children of George III.

Then it seems to have been lost sight of, or perhaps was mistaken for a punch bowl, for we find that in 1840–41, Queen Victoria ordered a baptismal font to be made of silver-gilt, which is now at Windsor Castle, and in which all Princes and Princesses from that date have been baptised. It may confidently be hoped that at some future date the older font will again come into use, and will not again be lost to sight.

Charles II's font gives the general impression of a large, covered bowl standing on a slender, rounded column, and has a somewhat top-heavy effect. In height it is about 3 ft. 6 in., whilst the bowl is about 18 in. in diameter. On top of the cover is a group of gold figures representing St. Philip baptising the eunuch, whilst below is the cypher of Charles II surmounted by a Royal crown. The same device is repeated on the base of the font. As part of the set is a very handsome and massive golden alms dish with the Royal arms of the Stuarts engraved large in the centre.

The flagons which have become associated with this font are, as their plate-marks show, of later origin, and the association, therefore, was only temporary, and might without doubt be dissevered. They are, in fact, tankards made and intended to be used at the festal board, and not for sacramental wine. The designs in high relief on these tankards is sufficient evidence of this, for they depict bacchanalian scenes of the most realistic nature. It is possible that it was these flagons, which were thought to be indissoluble from the font, which caused the whole set to be put aside by Queen Victoria. The flagons are of German origin, made in

Hamburg, and though their date is uncertain, may rightly be ascribed to the Hanoverian dynasty.

Amongst the ecclesiastical plate is a very handsome golden alms dish and flagon made for William and Mary, the plate-marks on which show they were made in 1691–92. The alms dish is more than two feet in diameter, and has in the centre in high relief a fine representation of the Last Supper. Below this is a panel on which is displayed the cypher of William and Mary, surmounted by a royal crown. Round the wide rim, also in high relief, are four winged cherubs, and between these golden foliage, garlands, and fruit. The flagon stands about a foot and a half high, and has a handle and cover. The body is covered with boldly embossed cherubs' faces, foliage, and festoons of roses and fruit. The cypher of William and Mary, surmounted by a royal crown, is on the front of the flagon.

These two pieces of ecclesiastical plate have the privilege of replacing much older plate three times a year on the altar of the Chapel of St. Peter ad Vincula within the Tower. These three occasions are Easter Sunday, Whit Sunday, and Christmas Day. On these three days the Keeper of the Jewel House hands them over to the Tower authorities for the period of morning service, and then, reclaiming them, replaces them with the Regalia.

The altar plate, which the alms dish and flagon of William and Mary replace on these three occasions, dates to the reigns of Charles I and Charles II. This older set of plate, though quite plain, is in the eyes of connoisseurs more impressive than the more ornate and finely designed insignia of the later reign. The origin of this curious routine is lost in antiquity. It may, however, have been ordered so as to emphasize the arrival of a new dynasty and the death of the old ; thus with large and resplendent plate to outshine the smaller and plainer vessels of the Stuarts. But the origin, be what it may, the custom has become established, and will without doubt continue year by year as long as the Tower stands, and England is England.

CHAPTER VI

THE REGAL EMBLEMS

The emblems of Royalty—Spiritual and Temporal—The regalia used at the Coronation of George V—The emblems borne in procession at Westminster—The Ampulla or golden eagle—The Anointing Spoon—The Sword and Spurs—The ceremony of the Jewelled Sword—The King offers it to the Church—Redeems it for 100 shillings—The Armilla, or Pall of Cloth of Gold—The Orb placed in the King's hand—A potent of Christian domination—The Coronation ring—The ensign of Kingly Dignity—The Sceptre with the Cross—The Sceptre with the Dove—A glove presented by the Lord of the Manor of Worksop—The King is crowned with St. Edward's Crown—The Peers put on their coronets—the people shout and "the great guns of the Tower are shot off "—The enthronement of the King—The Queen's Coronation—The Anointing—The Ring—The Queen is crowned—The Peeresses put on their coronets—The Queen's Sceptre— The Ivory Rod with the Dove—The Regal emblems on view in the Tower.

THE emblems of Royalty are many and curious, and each has its significance. When a King or Queen of England is crowned, all these emblems are brought from the Tower to Westminster Abbey, and each in turn is presented to the new sovereign by the Archbishop of Canterbury. This fact in itself is curious and interesting. It is not the House of Lords which represents the aristocracy of the country, nor the

House of Commons which represents the people, nor the Lord Chancellor as representing Law and Order, but the highest prelate of the Church of England, the Archbishop of Canterbury, who on behalf of 500,000,000 subjects of every race and creed, is deputed to crown the rightful successor King of Great Britain and Ireland and Emperor of wide-world dominions.

Of these emblems some are of a purely kingly significance, such as the Crown and Sceptre; others, like the Orb and Ring, have a religious connection, whilst others, as symbolized by the Sword and Spurs, are military emblems giving the knightly touch.

When a King or Queen is to be crowned, all the regal emblems from amongst the Crown Jewels, which are required for the ceremony, having been conveyed from the Tower to Westminster Abbey, are there met by the Peers and high officers, each of whom, either by hereditary right or by order of the King, takes charge of one emblem. The portions of the regalia used at the Coronation of King George V were :

St. Edward's Crown, or the Crown of England.
The King's Imperial State Crown.
The Orb.
The Sceptre with the Cross.
The Sceptre with the Dove.
The Jewelled State Sword.

F

The Sword of State.

The Three Swords of Justice and Mercy.

The Gold Spurs of St. George.

The Bracelets.

The Coronation Ring.

The Ampulla or Golden Eagle.

The Anointing Spoon.

These are all borne in procession to the altar, and there, with the exception of the Swords, each article is handed to the Archbishop of Canterbury, who in his turn hands them to the Dean of Westminster, and by that prelate they are each in due order placed upon the altar. When the ceremony of coronation commences, the first emblems used are the Ampulla and Spoon.

The Dean of Westminster pours a little of the oil from the Ampulla into the Anointing Spoon and takes it to the Archbishop. The Archbishop dips his first two fingers into the oil, and with the oil that adheres to them anoints the King, first on the head, then on the breast bared for the occasion, and thirdly on the palms of both hands. In each case the anointing is made in the form of a cross. This ceremony of the anointing of Kings is of very ancient origin, as may be gathered from Bible history. Thousands of years ago it was the custom to pour oil on the King's head and thus anoint him King over his people. What the origin of the custom was is not quite clear, but in the course of centuries it has become a recognized and indispensable part of the ceremony. Indeed, so indispensable, that there is on record a case where a Queen who had always been obliged to wear a wig was so impressed with the importance of the oil actually reaching the skin of her head that she had a small trap-door cut in the top of her wig so that the holy oil might assuredly reach its destination. In olden days the oil was literally poured on to the King's head, so that it ran down his beard and must have considerably damaged his clothes. In another place[1] is mentioned the old horn comb, used to rearrange the King's hair, perchance disordered by a too enthusiastic archbishop, which was thrown away by the Commonwealth.

The next portions of the Regalia which come into the ceremony are the Spurs and Sword, the emblems of knighthood and chivalry. With the Spurs the Lord Great Chamberlain merely touches the King's heels and returns them to the altar, but of the Sword much is made. It is in itself a magnificent work of art resplendent with costly jewels, the most valuable sword in the world. This most fittingly is carried by the Keeper of the Jewel House, an officer of high rank in the Army and a warrior of many wars. The Archbishop of Canterbury, taking the Sword, and accompanied by the Archbishop of York, the Bishops of London and Winchester

[1] See p. 96.

and other bishops assisting, approaches the King and delivers it into the King's right hand. And the King having girt the sword about him, the Archbishop gives him a benediction strongly reminiscent of that bestowed on the Knights of the Bath in olden days : " With this Sword do justice, stop the growth of iniquity, protect the Holy Church of God, help and defend widows and orphans, restore the things that are gone to decay, maintain the things that are restored, punish and reform what is amiss, and confirm what is in good order : that doing these things you may be glorious in all virtue ; and so faithfully serve our Lord Jesus Christ in this life, that you may reign for ever with Him in the life which is to come." This Jewelled Sword is then ungirded and placed by the King on the altar as his tribute to the Almighty, but the Almighty having no need of so valuable or indeed of any sword, it is redeemed by the Keeper of the Jewel House on payment of 100 shillings to the Archbishop, and returns eventually to safe keeping in the Tower.

The Dean of Westminster then puts upon the King the Armilla or stole, and the Imperial Mantle or Pall of Cloth of Gold, the Lord Great Chamberlain fastening the clasps.

The King being seated, the Archbishop of Canterbury places in his hand the Orb, which is the sign and portent of Christian dominion throughout the world.

On top of the Orb is a jewelled Cross standing on a great amethyst. To this the Archbishop draws attention, saying : "And when you see this Orb set under the Cross, remember that the whole world is subject to the Power and Empire of Christ our Redeemer." The Orb is then handed by the King to the Dean of Westminster, who again places it on the altar.

The Coronation Ring is the next emblem to be brought forward also by the Keeper of the Jewel House. The ring is the ensign of kingly dignity and of the defence of the Catholic faith, and is placed by the Archbishop on the fourth finger of His Majesty's right hand. The ring is of gold, and set therein is a large sapphire of great value surrounded by a circle of small diamonds. Across, but clear of the sapphire, north to south and east to west, are long, narrow rubies, giving the general effect of a red cross on a dark blue background, the Cross of St. George on a shield. A smaller replica of this large ring was given to Queen Victoria by William IV, and used at Her Majesty's Coronation. William IV naturally had this ring made in his lifetime when the Princess Victoria was young, but before the time that she came to the throne both she and her finger had grown larger. With many other things to think about, nobody thought of trying the ring on the Queen's finger before the ceremony, all taking it for granted that it had been

fitted. Hence resulted the historic struggle of the
Archbishop of Canterbury to thrust the ring on,
and the intense agony of Her Majesty throughout
the rest of the ceremony. Both of these may be
seen in the Jewel House, together with the ruby
ring described later.

Next in the ceremony comes the presentation to the
King of the Sceptre with the Cross, and the Sceptre
with the Dove. But before the Archbishop places
these in his hands, the Lord of the Manor of Worksop,
by ancient right, presents the King with a glove
which His Majesty draws on. The Lord of the Manor
of Worksop also has the privilege of supporting the
King's right arm after the Sceptre has been placed
in the King's hand. The Sceptre with the Cross,
which is the ensign of kingly power and justice, is
delivered into the King's right hand by the Archbishop. This is the sceptre which has the great
diamond the Star of South Africa set in its head.
This addition, which was introduced in the reign
of Edward VII, was directly inspired by that wise
monarch. The diamond represented the latest and
youngest member of the British Empire, but the
King made the proviso that though the great
diamond was to be introduced no portion of the
ancient sceptre was to be cut away or destroyed.
When the King commands someone will be found
with the brains and ingenuity to follow out the
deep political sentiment thus expressed. The brains

THE KING'S ROYAL SCEPTRE.

Reproduced by permission of Messrs. Cassell & Co., from a painting made by
Mr. Cyril Davenport (*Copyright*).

and ingenuity were duly furnished by Garrard's, perhaps the most famous of a long succession of Court Jewellers.

The Sceptre with the Dove, which is known as the Rod of Equity and Mercy, is by the same prelate placed in the King's left hand.

The King holds these two sceptres in his hands, whilst the definite act of coronation takes place. The crown used is St. Edward's Crown, or the Crown of England. This the Archbishop first places on the altar, and pronounces a blessing. The Dean of Westminster than takes the crown and with the bishops processes towards the King, who is seated in the ancient Coronation Chair. There he hands the crown to the Archbishop, "who putteth it reverently on the King's head. At the sight thereof the people with loud and repeated shouts cry, "God save the King"; the Peers and the Kings of Arms put on their coronets, and the trumpets sound, and by a signal given the great guns of the Tower are shot off." [1]

St. Edward's Crown is very heavy, being made of massive gold; it is therefore almost immediately replaced by the King's State Crown, a much lighter and at the same time much more resplendent insignia. St. Edward's Crown is never used again till the next sovereign in succession comes to be crowned. Throughout his reign the King on all State occasions,

[1] From the Coronation Service.

such as the opening of Parliament, wears his State Crown, sometimes known as the Diamond Crown. Indeed, it may well be so called, for it is one great mass of brilliancy thrown forth by more than 6000 diamonds of every size.

The final act in the Coronation ceremony is the enthronement, or as it is more anciently named, the Inthronisation. Wearing the State Crown, with a sceptre in each hand, and clothed in the robes of majesty, the King is conducted from St. Edward's Chair to the Throne of England, and is placed upon it by the Archbishop of Canterbury. Then all those peers and high officers who bear the Swords, and Orb, and other portions of the Regalia, group themselves round the steps of the throne, whilst the Archbishop makes his final exhortation. After the coronation of a sovereign all the Regalia are handed back to the Keeper of the Jewel House and conveyed to the Tower of London, where the majority rest till the next King or Queen ascends the Throne.

During a reign the only portions of the Regalia which usually leave the Tower are the King's State Crown, the Queen's State Crown, the Sword of State, and such maces as are required, these being used when the King opens Parliament in State. On great occasions, however, such as the day when peace was declared, at the end of the Great War, the silver trumpets are taken out and the State trumpeters sound a fanfare thereon when the heralds make proclamation. At the same time two or three of the Sergeants-at-Arms' maces are also taken out and borne in the heralds' procession.

When a Queen in her own right, like Queen Victoria, is crowned, she uses the same Regalia as is above described for a King, but when the Queen is a Queen Consort the procedure and Regalia are different. For such occasions a double set are made, such as were used by James II and his Queen Mary of Modena; by William III and Mary II; by Edward VII and Queen Alexandra; and by George V and Queen Mary. The Regalia of a Queen Consort consists of a State Crown, a ring, and two sceptres, with regal robes somewhat similar to those of the King.

The ceremony of the coronation of a Queen Consort is comparatively brief, and is performed by the Archbishop of York. First the Queen is anointed, whilst four peeresses hold a rich pall or canopy of gold over her. The Archbishop is enjoined to pour the oil on Her Majesty's head, but we confidently hope that he is usually not too literal in the interpretation of this injunction. After the anointing, the Keeper of the Jewel House hands the Coronation Ring to the Archbishop, who places it on the Queen's fourth finger of the right hand, giving to it the name of the Seal of Faith. Then the Archbishop takes the Queen's Crown and reverently places it on her head, re-

ferring to it as the Crown of glory, honour, and joy.
At the same moment as the Queen is crowned all
the peeresses put on their coronets. Finally the
Archbishop of York places a Sceptre in the Queen's
right hand, and the Ivory Rod with the Dove in
her left hand.

All the regal emblems above described are kept
in the Jewel House at the Tower of London, and
are there on view every day in the week, except
Sundays and Christmas Day, all the year round.
On Saturdays and Bank Holidays the Jewel House
is free to visitors, whilst on other days a charge of
sixpence is made. On a Whit Monday Bank Holi-
day as many as 16,000 people have been known to
pass free through the Jewel House. The money
paid for entrance does not, as in the old days, go to
the Keeper of the Jewel House or to his assistants,
but to the Treasury. The takings vary from over
£700 in a good month, say August, down to £150
in a bad month, generally December. The total
fees taken must be some £5000 per annum. Thus
the Crown Jewels are not like talents hidden in the
ground, but bring in a handsome income to the
State.

CHAPTER VII

THE GREAT TRAGEDY

Tragedy comes to the Crown Jewels—The Parliamentary obsession
—The emblems of royalty to be destroyed—Some sensible
Lords—The Puritan unmasked—Some excellent bargains for
the righteous—The Black Prince's ruby sold for £4—Concealed
and returned to Charles II—Alfred the Great's Crown melted
down—Then 800 years old—Fetched £238—Queen Edith's
Crown—Sold for £16—A glass cup for £102—The golden Dove,
emblematic of the Holy Ghost, £26—The three swords another
bargain—St. George's gold spurs for £1 13s. 4d.—The "old
horne comb"—A complete list of the Royal plate and jewels
with their values—The Robes destroyed—The Restoration—
Regalia furnished for Charles II—Cost £320,000 of our money—
Included therein "a paire of Trowses and breeches over them"—
The presents of plate—The city of Exeter's gift—And that of the
Borough of Plymouth—A wine fountain and its uses—The
Great Salts—A golden baptismal font—The pilfering of jewels
—James II pays £500 for hire of jewels at his coronation—
A new State Crown required—A diadem which cost £110,000—
A new Sceptre with the Dove £440—The Sceptre with the Cross
£1025—St. Edward's staff—A new Orb for Queen Mary of
Modena—The aquamarine monde of James II—The Maundy
Dish—The Alms Dish and flagon of William and Mary—The
Imperial Crown of India—Queen Mary's Crown—The tragedy
of 1649 happily wiped out.

THE greatest tragedy which has ever happened to the Crown Jewels occurred
during the sway of the Commonwealth.
This period, thus misappropriately named,
was, it is said by people who know all about these

things, merely a national aperient, which as such, they say, served its purpose, but the medicine smells no sweeter to many of us of this day than it did to those who had to swallow it in that bygone age. The Parliamentarians took themselves extremely seriously, and in the solemn attempt to stamp out the monarchy, and all monarchical principles, they with the limited intelligence that permeates the parochially-minded thought to further this fanatical principle by destroying even the emblems of royalty. This though these had become nothing more dangerous than any other articles of wondrous historic value such as are fitly preserved in the British Museum. This class of fanatic might, with ponderous conscientiousness, blow up the Pyramids of Egypt in furtherance of some similar principle.

In solemn conclave, therefore, the House of Commons passed a resolution that all emblems of royalty should be totally broken up, the gold and silver to be melted down, and the jewels sold to the best advantage. True there were a few sensible members of the House of Lords who pointed out that the historic value of the Crown Jewels far exceeded their intrinsic worth, and that to melt down crowns and plate and to disperse jewels of renown was a very extravagant procedure, especially so in an era of strict economy. Nevertheless, broken up and destroyed were the Crown Jewels, and happily we have a list of the portions which fell into the melting-pot, or beneath the hammer of the auctioneer. The House of Commons of those days was liberally primed with what are known as Puritans. A Puritan was doubtless an excellent person according to his lights, but an outside world has since been, perhaps unjustly, somewhat inclined to confound him with another not very popular and more ancient biblical type. It is, therefore, perhaps not unnatural to find that many mundane persons of those days, such as Royalists and Cavaliers, in whispers at the time and later more openly, declared that the disposal of the Crown Jewels was so effected as to give the Members of Parliament and their friends some very handsome bargains.

This, indeed, would not be difficult, for as a matter of policy it was considered inadvisable that any obtrusive popular rush should take place for the possession of these royalist relics. Rather was it endeavoured to demonstrate of what little value they were in the eyes of the simple Republican; therefore, doubtless the sale was little advertised. It would be very interesting to know, for instance, who and how some lucky person secured the Black Prince's ruby, which is, and was, practically priceless, for £4. It may, of course, have been a Royalist who obtained possession, and who, guarding it carefully, handed it back to Charles II on his Restoration. We should like to think so. But more probably it went at that bargain price to a friend of Parliament, and by him was preserved as a good investment, and eventually was sold back for money, or a substantial benefit, to Charles II. All that really matters now is that the ruby survived those troublous days, and found itself again in a place of honour in the State Crown of Charles II.

An object of great interest which was melted down was the Crown of Alfred the Great. This was made of gold wire-work, set with small gems, and weighed 79½ ounces. Even at that time it was nearly 800 years old. Melted down, this crown was sold at £3 an ounce, and fetched altogether £238 10s. 0d. What became of the stones is not stated. Either the despoilers had a disappointment in the Crown of Queen Edith, wife of King Harold, or its value was of set purpose depreciated. This crown had always been held to be of massive gold, but the assayers, it is said, found that it was made only of silver-gilt, but it was set with garnets, pearls, sapphires, and other stones. It weighed 50½ ounces, and was sold for £16 only. This appears to have been a good investment for the fortunate purchaser.

The " large glass cup wrought in figures," which is mentioned in the inventory as having been sold for £102 15s. 0d., was a very ancient and valuable article. It was not of glass, but was made of agate, and was the great " stone " chalice of Edward the Confessor. It is mentioned by Sporley, and was then six hundred years old, and the date of the sale is nearly three hundred years ago. All trace of this chalice has been lost; it has probably long since been broken and thrown away, unknown and unhonoured.

Amongst the articles to be broken up or sold is a curious item. It is entered as " A dove of gold, set with stones, and pearle, poiz. 8½ ounces, in a box sett with studs of silver gilt." By some this has been confused with the ampulla or golden eagle, for a dove or an eagle when not very exactly made might resemble each other or any other bird. Very possibly the Parliamentary Commissioners did so mistake this dove for an eagle, and thought they were destroying the ampulla. This, however, as we have seen, was hidden away and escaped the general sacrilege and destruction. This dove was probably merely a holy emblem representing the Holy Ghost, as does the dove on the top of the sceptre.

Amongst the less valuable articles sold are mentioned three swords with scabbards of cloth of gold, which were disposed of for £1 each. Here again somebody secured a great bargain, for these three swords would in all probability be those sent to Henry VIII by the Pope, when he bestowed on that monarch the title of " Defender of the Faith." These three swords were reproduced from ancient drawings at the Restoration of Charles II, and are now preserved in the Jewel House. They are the swords of Justice, Temporal and Spiritual, and the Sword of Mercy. The point of this latter sword has been purposely broken off about six inches, as an emblem of mercy. The ultimate fate of three original swords is not known. Only a short time ago, however, three swords very like these were dug up at Mitcham when the foundations of a house were being prepared. This spot has long been known as the site of an ancient Anglo-Saxon settlement, and it is probable that there was still a hamlet here in Cromwellian days. It is, therefore, quite possible that someone bought or acquired the swords at the great dispersal, that their history got lost sight of, and that they were lost and buried amidst the natural decay which ordinary buildings suffer in the course of centuries.

One of the King's military emblems, St. George's Spurs, are mentioned as having been sold for £1 13s. 4d., they had always been held to be of pure gold, but were sold as silver gilt.

Last of the list comes an almost pathetic article, to wit, one old horne comb " worth nothing." This was probably the comb which may have been used for centuries, and by many Kings, to rearrange their hair after the Archbishop had perchance disturbed it when anointing His Majesty's head at the coronation.

A list of the chief portions of Regalia, broken up and sold by order of Parliament, with the prices realised, mentioned in *The Crown Jewels of England*,[1] may be of interest :—

" A true and perfect Inventory of all the plate and jewells now being in the upper Jewell-house of the Tower, in the charge of Sir Henry Mildmay, together with an appraisement of them, made and taken the 13th, 14th, and 15th daies of August, 1649 :

The Imperial crowne of massy gold, weighing 7 lbs. 6 oz., valued at	£1110	0	0
The queenes crowne of massy gold, weighing 3 lbs. 10 oz.,	£338	3	4
A small crowne found in an iron chest, formerly in the Lord Cottington's charge (from other accounts this appears to have been the crown of Edward VI.),	£73	16	8
——the gold, the diamonds, rubies, sapphires, etc.,	£355	0	0
The globe, weighing 1 lb. 5¼ oz.,	£57	10	0
Two coronation bracelets, weighing 7 oz. (with three rubies and twelve pearls),	£36	0	0
Two sceptres, weighing 18 oz.,	£60	0	0
A long rodd of silver gilt, 1 lb. 5 oz.,	£4	10	8

[1] *The Crown Jewels of England*, by Major-General Sir George Younghusband and Cyril Davenport.

G

The foremention'd crownes, since yͤ inventorie was taken, are accordinge to ordͬ of parmͭ totallie broken and defaced.

The inventory of that part of the regalia which are now removed from Westminster Abbey to the Jewel House in the Tower.

Queene Edith's crowne, formerly thought to be of massy gould, but, upon trial, found to be of silver gilt ; enriched with garnetts, foule pearle, saphires and some odd stones, poiz. 50½ oz., valued at . . . £16 0 0

King Alfred's crowne of goulde wyer worke, sett with slight stones, poiz. 79½ oz. at £3 per oz., ... £248 10 0

A goulde plate dish, enamelled, etc., ... £77 11 0

One large glass cupp, wrought in figures, etc., . . . £102 15 0

A dove of gould, sett with stones, and pearle, poiz. 8½ oz., in a box sett with studs of silver gilt, . £26 0 0

The gould and stones belonging to a collar of crimson and taffaty, etc., ... £18 15 0

One staff of black and white ivory,
with a dove on the top, with
binding and foote of goulde,   .   £4 10 0
A large staff with a dove on yᵉ top,
formerly thought to be all gould,
but upon triall found to be, the
lower part wood within and
silver gilt without,   .   .   £2 10 0
Two sceptᵐ one sett with pearles
and stones, the upper end gould,
the lower end silver. The other
silver gilt with a dove, formerly
thought gould,   .   .   £65 16 10½
One silver spoone gilt, poiz. 3 oz., .   £0 16 0
The gould of the tassels of the livor
cull'd robe, weighing 4 oz.,
valued at £8, and the coat with
the neck button of gould, £2,
the robe having some pearle,
valued at £3, in all   .   .   £13 0 0
One paire of silver gilt spurres,
etc., ...   £1 13 4

All these according to order of Parliament are
broken and defaced."

The ancient coronation robes destroyed at the same time are catalogued and valued as follows :—

" One common taffaty robe, very old, valued at . . .	£0	10	0
One robe, laced with goulde lace, .	£0	10	0
One livor cull^ed silk robe, very old and worth nothing, . .	£0	0	0
One robe of crimson taffaty, sarcenett valued at . .	£0	5	0
One paire of buskins, cloth of silver and silver stockings, very old, and valued at . .	£0	2	6
One paire of shoes of cloth of gold, at	£0	2	6
One paire of gloves embroid^ed wth gould, at . . .	£0	1	0
Three swords with scabbards of cloth of goulde, at . .	£3	0	0
One old combe of horne, worth nothing, . . .	£0	0	0
Total in the chest, . .	£4	11	0"

The old Regalia having thus been wantonly destroyed, it became necessary when the monarchy was restored to make anew the emblems of royalty. This work was entrusted to Sir Robert Vyner, the Court Jeweller, with instructions that he was to follow as closely as possible the fashions of those destroyed.

The order included two crowns, one the Crown of England, known as St. Edward's Crown, with which the King was to be crowned, and the other a State Crown which the King in accordance with ancient custom would wear on all other State occasions during his reign. Two sceptres also were to be made, one the Sceptre with the Cross and the other the Sceptre with the Dove. The Orb of gold set with jewels and surmounted by a cross came next ; then St. Edward's Staff, which is to guide the King's footsteps,' and the Armilla[1] and Ampulla.[2] The bill for these, together with some minor portions of the Regalia, amounted to £32,000, or about £320,000 at the present purchasing value of the sovereign.

Sir Edward Walker, Garter Principal King-at Arms in the reign of Charles II, gives an interesting and detailed account of this restoration of the Regalia.[3]

" Because through the Rapine of the late unhappy times, all the Royall Ornaments and Regalia heretofore preserved from age to age in the Treasury of the Church at Westminster, were taken away, sold and destroyed, the Committee mett divers

---

[1] A stole made of cloth of gold.   [2] See p. 73.
[3] *The Crown Jewels of England*, by Younghusband and Davenport.

times not only to direct the remaking such Royall Ornaments and Regalia, but even to sette the form and fashion of each particular : all which doe now retayne the old names and fashion, although they have been newly made and prepared by orders given to the Earle of Sandwich, Master of the Great Wardrobe, and Sr Gilbert Talbott, Kn^t., Master of the Jewell House.

Hereupon the Master of the Jewell House had order to provide two Imperial Crownes sett with pretious Stones, the one to be called St. Edward's Crowne, wherewith the king was to be crowned, and the other to be putt on after his Coronation, before his Maties retorne to Westminster Hall. Also

An Orbe of Gold with a Crosse sett with pretious Stones.

A Scepter with a Crosse sett with pretious Stones, called St. Edward's.

A Scepter with a Dove sett with pretious Stones.

A long Scepter, or Staffe of Gold with a Crosse upon the top, and a Pike at the foote of steele, called St. Edward's staffe.

A Ring with a Ruby.

A Paire of Gold Spurrs.

A Chalice, and Paten of Gold.

An Ampull for the Oyle and a spoone.

And two Ingotts of Gold, the one a pound and the other a marke for the King's 2 Offerings."

Besides these obvious tokens of royalty there were and are a host of minor insignia which take their part in the Coronation ceremony, down to the garments which the King wears next his person. Amongst these appears a shirt of fine linen, to be left open in the place where the Archbishop would anoint the King. The Master of the Great Wardrobe had also to produce "a paire of Trowses, and Breeches over them, with Stockings fastened to the Trowses, all of Crimson Silke"; and amongst other things a pair of linen gloves, which appear very modestly amidst so much splendour.

To supplement these strictly regal emblems the people came forth gladly with offers of plate to replace what had been melted down. As the solitary piece of plate, left no doubt by an oversight by the despoilers, was Queen Elizabeth's gold salt cellar, which is now in the Tower, much had to be supplied to set the Royal table again on a regal scale. Devonshire, as we have seen, came forth nobly in the cause, the two finest pieces of plate coming from the loyal citizens of Exeter and Plymouth. Exeter presented a State salt cellar, described in a former chapter, and the Borough of Plymouth supplied the wine fountain already described, both well in keeping with the jovial days which wiped out the recollection of the dismal period of the Commonwealth. It is a genial picture to imagine King Charles with his jovial courtiers stemming the tide set loose by the loyal

Borough of Plymouth, and taking salt with his almonds out of the Great Salt.

In accordance with the fashion of the age, the plate on a dinner-table appears to have consisted very largely of great salt cellars. These were made of great size, so that besides furnishing a modicum of salt, which was a precious thing in those days, they gave a rich tone to the festive board. In the Jewel House are no less than eleven of these great gold salt cellars, all of which are known as St. George's Salts, and all of which formed a portion of the Royal Plate of Charles II.

To that popular monarch was also presented a gold christening font, with the hope shared by all his loyal subjects that many children of His Majesty would be christened from it. The fates decided otherwise, but the font remained a Royal font, and many infant princes and princesses were christened in it up to the days of Queen Victoria.

The Regalia seems to have been somewhat hardly used in Charles II's reign, or Sir Gilbert Talbot, the Keeper, must have much neglected his charge. Doubtless a good deal of damage was done to the State Crown and the Orb, and also to the Sceptre, when Colonel Blood tried to carry them off. Several stones were then lost, we know, but that would not account for the heavy bill which had to be paid when James II came to the throne.

The Crown of England, known as St. Edward's

Crown, which had been new made for Charles II, and should never have left the Jewel House in the Tower until the next King was crowned, had evidently had the valuable stones pilfered out of it and worthless imitations set in their places. To replace these gems appears to have been beyond the finances of James II and his Parliament, for it is on record that the sum of £500 was paid for the *hire* of jewels for the Coronation ceremony, probably from the Court Jewellers. In addition, £350 was paid for additional gold and workmanship.

Apparently, too, the State Crown of Charles II, which had been battered in by Colonel Blood, was not in serviceable condition, for a new one had to be made at a cost of £7870. Many of the old gems, including the Black Prince's ruby, were doubtless used, but the bill mentions that it includes fresh jewels. The Crown and Diadem of his Queen, Mary of Modena, are not mentioned in this bill; the cost of these may therefore have been otherwise defrayed, possibly by the King out of his Privy Purse. Both are now in the Jewel House, and the diadem alone is said to have cost £110,000, a very large sum indeed in those days.

A new Sceptre with the Dove was made, richly jewelled, and costing £440; as well as a Sceptre with the Cross, at a cost of £1025. Both of these were probably made for Mary of Modena, and may be seen amongst the present Regalia. St. Edward's

Staff, costing £225, is also charged for, though one had been made for Charles II, and this latter is in the Tower. Also appears in the list one Orb, costing £1150, probably made for Queen Mary of Modena, and now in the Jewel House. A pair of gold spurs, known as St. George's Spurs, are shown as supplied, the price being £63 7s. 6d. For the bracelets the charge appears to have been £44 18s. 6d., and for a chalice and palten £277 6s. 3d. These latter are not to be found in the Jewel House now.

The bill also includes repairs to the Ampulla, or Eaglet of Gold, and the Anointing Spoon, for which the charge is £102 5s. od. for the ampulla, and £2 for the spoon. The total bill for these items comes out to the handsome figure of £12,050 3s. 5d. Whoever made out this bill, and whichever Keeper signed it, must have known that they had a very complacent Treasury to deal with. St. Edward's Staff, the gold spurs, the gold bracelets, are all charged for, though they had already been made and presumably paid for in the previous reign. The ampulla, too, had been repaired and restored by Sir Robert Vyner only a few years before. All these, which to-day are in the Tower, seem to bear silent witness that somebody was paid twice over.

What James II said to Sir Gilbert Talbot over this, or what reply Sir Gilbert Talbot made to His Majesty, history does not relate. But the whole incident shows how very loosely kept were the Crown Jewels as recently as three hundred years ago. Indeed, to be strictly just, they were never really secure till the reign of Edward VII, and in the intervening centuries a fairly regular disappearance of gems and their replacement with coloured glass seems to have been the rule rather than the exception.

A piece of ecclesiastical plate added to the Royal treasure in the reign of Charles II was the Maundy Dish,[1] from which the Maundy money has since that reign been distributed on Maundy Thursday, the day before Good Friday. William and Mary have inscribed their monogram and crest on the dish, but the plate-mark shows that it belonged to the reign of Charles II.

Two other pieces of church plate which were added by William and Mary are a very handsome alms dish and flagon.[2] These have W.M. for William and Mary, surmounted by a crown embossed on them.

King George V and Queen Mary have added two of the finest and most important additions to the Regalia. These are the Imperial Crown of India and, Queen Mary's State Crown, which have already been fully described.

Thus, though it has taken some centuries to accomplish, the devastation wrought by the Commonwealth on the Regalia has been more than repaired. The Crown Jewels of the King of England are at this

[1] See p. 74.   [2] See p. 78.

time more magnificent and of far greater value than they have been in any former reign—nay more, they are of greater value both historically and intrinsically than the Crown Jewels of any other monarch.

THE KEEPER OF THE JEWEL HOUSE IN HIS STATE ROBES

CHAPTER VIII

THE KEEPERS OF THE JEWEL HOUSE

One of the most ancient offices under the Crown—The first keepers the Abbot and monks of Westminster, 1042—First official Keeper appointed in 1216 by Henry III—Jewels removed to the Tower—The Bishop of Carlisle as Keeper—John de Flete— Robert de Mildenhall—Thomas Cromwell, Earl of Essex— His romantic rise—A protégé of Cardinal Wolsey—Helps Henry VIII to divorce Katherine of Aragon—And to marry Anne Boleyn—Made Keeper of the Jewel House, 1532—In his port- folio found the famous letter of Anne Boleyn to Henry VIII— Executed on Tower Hill, 1540—The Marquis Winchester— His great rise—Keeper of the Jewels to Edward VI—Hands them to Lady Jane Grey as Queen—Escapes the block and is taken into favour by Queen Mary—Queen Elizabeth also renews these favours—Dies in his bed—Sir Henry Mildmay, Keeper of the Regalia in the reigns of James I, Charles I, and interregnum—Deserts King Charles and joins the Parliamentar- ians—One of the judges at Charles I's trial—Grows rich on the proceeds of his office—Dubbed " The Knave of Diamonds " —His flight, capture, and trial—His sentence—His estate confiscated and given to James, Duke of York—His picture after death—Sir Gilbert Talbot appointed by Charles II— His rights and perquisites—Holds the office for thirty years— Sir Francis Lawley—Heneage Montague—Charles Godfrey— Hon. James Brudenell—Lord Lynn—Lord Abergavenny— Lord Glenorchie—Sir Richard Lyttleton—The Earl of Darling- ton—A break in the ancient office in 1782—Revived in the nineteenth century—Lieut.-Col. Charles Wyndham, who charged with the Scots Greys at Waterloo—Sir Michael Biddulph— Sir Hugh Gough—Sir Robert Low—Sir Arthur Wynne.

ONE of the most ancient offices in the realm is that of Keeper of the Jewel House. His title has varied backwards and for- wards during the centuries ; at one time and in one reign he has been named the Master and Treasurer of the Jewel House, in another reign or century the Keeper of the Crown Jewels, sometimes he has been entitled the Keeper of the Regalia, and at others, as at present, the Keeper of the Jewel House, but his duties have been always the same, the custody of the Crown Jewels.

In very ancient days, when the emblems of royalty were few and of no great value, it was not necessary to have an officer especially appointed to guard them ; the Master of the King's Wardrobe would take them in charge along with the rich robes that a King wore in those days. So that it is not till 1042 that we hear definitely of anybody being placed in special charge of the King's Regalia.

The English King who first found it requisite and advisable to place his treasure under special guardianship was Edward the Confessor, and he, being inclined that way, placed it in charge of the Church. It was thus that the Abbot and monks of Westminster became the first Keepers of the Regalia some nine centuries ago. For nearly two hundred years the Abbey of Westminster safely kept its watch and ward, and it was only in 1216, in the reign of Henry III, that the most valuable portions of the Regalia, such as the Crown and Sceptre, were removed to the Tower of London.

The inadvisability in this sinful world of leaving Crown Jewels, intrinsically and historically of great value, only spiritually guarded, was brought into prominence by the theft of certain pieces of Royal plate by the monks in charge. With the removal of the Jewels to the Tower was appointed the first official Keeper. Who he was is not related, but a few years later, under the same monarch, it is clear that the Bishop of Carlisle held the post.

The Bishop was typical of that age, a man of the world, politician, courtier, with an episcopal mitre as an adjunct, or rather as a powerful auxiliary in his dealings with the world in general, and his King and fellow-subjects in particular. There is no record of the Bishop of Carlisle actually heading a charge of cavalry, as did Thomas à Becket in one of his less clerical moments, but he followed the King in his campaigns, whether as a strategical, tactical, political, or spiritual supporter, or whether in all four capacities, careful readers of the history of those days will be able to judge. But whatever his chief rôle or whatever the emoluments of his office, no mean addition came to his purse from the ancient rights and perquisites of the Keeper of the Jewel House.

Amongst the earlier keepers was John de Flete, who held the post in 1337 in the reign of Edward III, and whose pay we learn was twelve pence per diem. Ten years later, also during the reign of Edward III, Robert de Mildenhall was in custody of the Regalia; whilst in 1418 Henry VI appointed Thomas Chitterne.

None of these appear to have been men of any mark, but no doubt honest folks of good repute and good family, who could afford to live comfortably on the income derivable, without having other offices attached to it.

In the reign of Henry VIII we find that the highest officers in the State were appointed Keepers of the Regalia in addition to their more important duties. Amongst these was Thomas Cromwell, Earl of Essex, who, from very small beginnings, rose to be the most powerful personage in the State, only second to his sovereign. Son of a man of humble position, who combined the trade of butcher with that of shearer of cloth at Putney, he, after a turbulent youth at home and abroad, returned with empty pockets to the parental roof at the age of twenty-eight. He then married a lady of equally modest position, and settled down as a combined solicitor and shearer, concerning which combination of professions no doubt there passed a fairly obvious if rude jibe. As law and trade prospered, he moved first to Fenchurch Street and then to Austin Friars.

Thomas Cromwell's rise to fame commenced in 1523 when he became a protégé of Cardinal Wolsey, by whose influence he was returned for a seat in Parliament. He was a useful man, the Cardinal found, with a working knowledge both of the law and of business, whilst undoubtedly he was above the average in ability. Moreover he had the best of manners, acquired not only from his distinguished clients, but from his experiences abroad. This legal knowledge and these persuasive manners the Cardinal first put to useful service in suppressing the small monasteries, so as to secure funds for the endowment of colleges at Oxford and Ipswich. Wolsey was a great man, and the idea was great and good, but unfortunately the desired result had to be attained by the dubious method of violent despoilation. So entirely had Cromwell become agent for the Cardinal, that Anne Boleyn in a letter addresses him as the " Secretary of My Lord."

For five years Cromwell was the faithful servitor of the Cardinal, and then came the fall of that high potentate, a crash which threatened to bring to earth his follower with him. But Cromwell was an exceedingly clever person, and in the Commons succeeded in most ably defending his patron without offending his opponents or the King. By thus securing for his great patron a comparatively easy downfall, he added greatly to his own prestige. Wolsey escaped banishment or the block by acknowledging his misdeameanours and consenting to hand over the whole of his property to the King. The King in return for this princely endowment, which included Hampton Court much as we now see it, pensioned the great man off as Archbishop of York, in which seclusion he died two years later.

Cromwell had now caught the King's eye, and he

H

used his legal knowledge and acquired Court experience to climb the ladder, lately so nearly overturned. The King wished much to divorce Katherine of Aragon, and to marry Anne Boleyn, but the Pope stood in the way. Cromwell, the lawyer, suggested that as no legal obstacles stood in the way of the King, who can do no wrong, the simplest way of disposing of the religious difficulties was to deny the supremacy of the Pope in England and to proclaim himself head of the Church in his own land. Henry VIII followed this advice, threw the Pope overboard, divorced Katherine of Aragon, and married Anne Boleyn.

Naturally these great personal services went not unrewarded, first in his appointment as a Privy Councillor, and next as Keeper of the Jewel House, on April 14th, 1532. The latter was one of the substantial benefits which in pay and perquisites made a man rich in those days. His growing wealth and importance clearly pointed to the enlargement of his house and property at Austin Friars. It is curious to learn that what is thought a modern invention, the moving of a whole house on rollers, was employed by Cromwell nearly four centuries ago. A house belonging to a Mr. Stow was deemed to be inconveniently close to the Cromwellian mansion, so it was with or without consent jacked up on to rollers and bodily moved away to a less objectionable propinquity.

His part in securing the divorce of Katherine of Aragon and the succession of Anne Boleyn brought him still further quick and plenteous rewards. In rapid succession he became Lord Chancellor, the King's Secretary, Master of Rolls, and lastly Vicar-General, so that he might be in a position to enforce the supremacy of his King over the Church. Sir Thomas More, late Chancellor, and Bishop Fisher, fell beneath the axe on Cromwell's prosecution, their crime being a refusal to acknowledge the King's spiritual supremacy.

A little later we find Cromwell one of those who on the fatal May 2nd, 1536, escorted the Queen he had helped to make, the hapless Anne Boleyn, to the Tower. And only a few days later we see him seated a witness at her execution. In his portfolio was later found that most pathetic and well-known letter addressed by Anne Boleyn to the King [1] praying for mercy, which letter was never passed on to the King.

For four more years the sun shone on the erstwhile solicitor and shearer, and he became first a Knight of the Garter, then a Baron and Lord Great Chamberlain, and finally Earl of Essex. Great riches and territory too came to him from the suppression of the greater monasteries and the confiscation of their property. But in 1540 the sun set on this phenomenal career, for on June 10th

[1] See Appendix.

of that year, accused of high treason by the Duke of Norfolk, attainted by Parliament, he passed silently to that same block on Tower Hill to which he had assigned so many.

In the days when great officers of State held the lucrative office of Keeper of the Jewel House in addition to their other benefices was one William Paulet, who later became 1st Marquis of Winchester. Of good birth and a country squire, he was knighted in 1525, and the same year made a Privy Councillor. Shortly after he became a Member of Parliament as Knight of the shire of Hampshire, and also secured the curious appointment of "Surveyor of the King's widows, and Governor of all idiots and naturals in the King's hands." This apparently led by easy degrees to Controller of the Royal Household. In 1536 Sir William Paulet was one of the judges at the trials of Sir Thomas More, and Bishop Fisher, and also of the gentlemen with whom Queen Anne Boleyn was accused of too familiar consort.

A year later the Knight became a Baron, under the title of Lord St. John, and Treasurer of the Royal Household, whilst not long after he became a Knight of the Garter and Lord Chamberlain. When Henry VIII died he was Lord President of the Council, and must have sincerely thanked God that he had so far survived and prospered and had seen the end of that monarch's reign, with his head

THOMAS CROMWELL, EARL OF ESSEX
KEEPER OF THE JEWEL HOUSE IN THE REIGN OF HENRY VIII

still on his shoulders. The Lord President was one of the eighteen executors of Henry VIII's will, appointed to act as a council of regency during the minority of the boy King, Edward VI. In 1550 St. John sided with the Duke of Northumberland in the overthrow of Somerset, the Lord Protector, and as a result found himself on the winning side with an earldom, that of Wiltshire thrown in. He received also the offices of Lord Treasurer and Keeper of the Jewel House. A year later we find plain William Paulet of a few years ago created Marquis of Winchester.

When Edward VI died, the Marquis, as Keeper of the Jewel House, handed over the Crown Jewels to Lady Jane Grey, and saluted her as Queen. Nine days later, however, he was amongst the Lords who from Barnard's Castle, which lay on the river-bank close alongside the Tower, proclaimed Queen Mary the rightful sovereign of these realms. Nor did the new Queen resent the late temporary aberration, but took him to her stony heart, and not only confirmed him in all his offices, but added that of Lord Privy Seal. The Marquis was really a wonderful person, for though his next appearance in history is as one of those who conducted the Princess Elizabeth to the dread doom of imprisonment in the Tower, we next discover him, a man well stricken in years, riding through London proclaiming the same princess Queen of England. Nor

did Queen Elizabeth at once say, " Off with his
head " ; on the contrary, she confirmed him in his
appointment of Lord Treasurer. Though now
upwards of seventy years of age he was made
Speaker of the House of Lords, and died in harness
in 1572 at the venerable age of eighty-seven. The
secret of this long life, apart from physical fitness,
was the possession of the gift which perhaps we now
call tact. If any proof were needed, it is only
necessary to record that a plain squire rose to be a
marquis and lived through four reigns during which
heads fell as plentifully as apples in an autumn
gale, and yet eventually died peacefully in his bed.

One of the best known Keepers of the Crown
Jewels is Sir Henry Mildmay, who was appointed
to the office in April, 1620, by James I, and retained
that office not only through the reign of Charles I,
but also through the Commonwealth, and was only
dispossessed of it by Charles II on his Restoration in
1660. Besides being Keeper, or as he was termed
Master and Treasurer of the Jewel House, Sir
Henry was a Member of Parliament for Westbury
in Wiltshire, and also at another period for Maldon
in Essex. He was a *persona grata* with James I,
and also, it would seem, with Charles I during the
first fifteen years of his reign. But Sir Henry then
forsook his sovereign and became one of the Committee of the Commons. His defection was considered so important that he was, by the Parlia-

mentarians, continued in his office, in so far as concerned the drawing of the salary and emoluments thereof, though the situation was somewhat grotesque since he was of the party which was in open arms against the King, whose Crown Jewels he was supposed to guard.

Sir Henry was nominated, and sat as one of the judges who tried Charles I, but he with some courage or address escaped signing the death sentence, and afterwards claimed that he only accepted nomination in hopes of saving the King. Throughout the Commonwealth he remained Keeper of the Jewel House, though there were no jewels to guard, for these had been broken up, defaced, destroyed, and sold by the order of Parliament. But being one skilled in the etiquette of courts, he made himself useful as Master of Ceremonies to Foreign Ambassadors, and continued to enjoy the rich perquisites attaining to the office of Keeper of the Jewel House.

For forty years Sir Henry Mildmay had grown fat and prosperous on the proceeds of his office; indeed, he became a very rich man with great estates and much ready cash to spend. But in 1660 Charles II was restored to the throne, and Sir Henry Mildmay was immediately pounced upon to produce the crowns and robes, sceptres, and jewels belonging to the kingly dignity, of which he was the reputed guardian. At the time the general impression was that Sir Henry had appropriated these to his own purposes and sold them to his own advantage ; he was in consequence dubbed " the Knave of Diamonds." As however has since become clear the royal emblems, or such as remained, were disposed of under the orders of Parliament. It may, however, be conjectured that Sir Henry, in accordance with the usages of the age and the rights of his office, secured a goodly percentage on the sale prices. His detractors averred that he had himself valued and bought in the Crown Jewels at the exceedingly low prices they fetched, and at his leisure disposed of them at great profit. There is, however, no recorded proof of this.

But Sir Henry Mildmay, whether he had a guilty conscience or not, thought discretion the better part of valour, and attempted to escape abroad. He was, however, caught by Lord Winchelsea at Rye in Essex and sent back to London. He was tried in 1661 at the Bar of the House of Commons, and sentenced to be degraded from all his honours and titles. Furthermore, he was sentenced to be annually drawn on a hurdle through the streets of London from the Tower to Tyburn, then passed under the gallows, and again dragged back to the Tower. This penalty was to be exacted on each anniversary of the day on which sentence had been passed on Charles I, that is January 27th. Whether Sir Henry ever took this ride is not clear, but probably he did more than once, for it was only in 1664 that the

Lords in mitigation ordered him to be transported to Tangiers. On the way to his exile, however, he died at the town of Antwerp. His vast accumulations of wealth were forfeited to the Crown, his estate at Wanstead being of sufficient importance to be assigned to James, Duke of York.

There was a strong rumour at the time that Sir Henry Mildmay had been either hanged or beheaded, which rumour caused his relations and descendants great annoyance. As proof to the contrary they produced a painting of the dead knight, which still exists, showing him lying on his back on his death-bed. The clothes have been drawn down and his neck bared, so as to clearly show that no trace of cord or axe was upon it, and that he died no felon's death. Naturally a picture of this sort is no proof in a court of law, for the artist might with ease omit all signs of violence; but history bears out the contention that Sir Henry Mildmay died a natural death.

Whatever the merits or demerits of Sir Henry Mildmay may have been, Charles II had too many Royalists with claims on his generosity to retain in office one who had evidently been hand-in-glove with those who had kept the King from his father's throne, and in exile for so long. Amongst those with such a claim was Sir Gilbert Talbot, who had followed the King's fortunes in France, and was now back in England in impoverished circum-

stances. On his application for an appointment
the King made him Keeper, or as he was then styled,
Master and Treasurer of the Jewel House. We are
indebted to a very interesting manuscript dictated
in 1680 by Sir Gilbert Talbot for a detailed account
of the ancient rights and perquisites belonging to the
office. These he obtained from Sir Henry Mildmay,
and it is expressly stated that they were the same
as enjoyed by Thomas Cromwell, Earl of Essex,
in the reign of Henry VIII. Facsimiles of some of
the pages of the manuscript are given, but it is of
historic interest that they should be recorded in
full, and these will be found in the Appendix. Sir
Gilbert Talbot held the office for thirty-one years,
and as is duly related elsewhere, was in office when
Colonel Blood made his attempt to steal the Crown
and other portions of the Regalia. Sir Gilbert and
his connection with his office enters so much into
other parts of this book that it is not necessary here
to say more about him.

When Sir Gilbert Talbot died in 1691 the office of
Master and Treasurer of the Jewel House fell in
succession to persons of various degrees and ranks,
of whom little can be gathered from modern books
of reference.

Sir Francis Lawley, doubtless an ancestor of the
present Lawleys, was next in charge of the Crown
Jewels for six years, and was succeeded by Heneage
Montague, probably a cadet of the family of

Montagu, who a few years later became Duke of Manchester.

Montague was followed by Charles Godfrey, who was Keeper through parts of three reigns, those of William and Mary, Anne, and George I. Then came the Hon. James Brudenell, a son of Lord Brudenell, a title now merged into that of the Marquis of Ailesbury, who held the office for fourteen years during the reigns of George I and George II. The Hon. James Brudenell was succeeded by Charles Townshend, Lord Lynn, who was nine years Keeper in the reign of George II.

The next in succession was William Neville, Lord Abergavenny, an ancestor of the present Marquis of Abergavenny, though the family now spells the name Nevill without the final " e." This Keeper was in office for six years in the reign of George II.

He was succeeded by John Campbell, Lord Glenorchie,[1] a son of the Earl of Breadalbane, who had custody of the Crown Jewels for eleven years in the reign of George III. Next in succession came Sir Richard Lyttleton, who held sway for thirteen years and through parts of two reigns. Next came Henry Vane, Earl of Darlington, who retained the post for close on twenty years. Whether this nobleman was inefficient, or eventually suffered from senile decay, is not recorded, but evidently a Keeper was

[1] Now spelt Glenorchy.

deemed a superfluous person, for on his death came a break in the ancient office which had then existed for seven hundred years, and even through so unfavourable a period for Royal offices as the Commonwealth.

When Lord Darlington died in 1782 the office of Keeper of the Regalia was suppressed under an Act of Parliament, known as Stat. 22 Geo. III, c. 82, and his duties were transferred to the Lord Chamberlain. It is reasonable to conjecture that the pay and perquisites also went to the Lord Chamberlain.

For forty years or more the office of Keeper lay dormant, whilst the Lord Chamberlain remained responsible for the safety of the Crown Jewels. It was not indeed till the reign of Queen Victoria that the question arose of the suitability of this arrangement, for naturally the Lord Chamberlain has much else to do, and cannot give his personal guardianship to so great a responsibility. It was the Duke of Wellington, who was then Constable of the Tower, who brought the matter to Her Majesty's notice, and Queen Victoria thereupon decided to revive the office of Keeper of the Crown Jewels. Appropriately, too, Her Majesty decided that in future this charge should be entrusted to an old and valiant soldier. Her first choice, therefore, was Lieut.-Colonel Charles Wyndham, who had charged with the Scots Greys at the Battle of Waterloo, and is, it is said, one of those portrayed in the famous and historic painting by Lady Butler, known all over the world, " Scotland for Ever."

No less than seven officers were one after another appointed by Queen Victoria during her long reign, each serving till he died or was promoted elsewhere. Colonel John Cox Gawler, late 73rd Foot, succeeded Colonel Wyndham, and was in his turn succeeded by Captain Arthur John Loftus, late 10th Hussars. Then came Lieut.-General Sir Michael Biddulph, G.C.B., a very distinguished officer who, after a few years as Keeper of the Crown Jewels, was transferred to the House of Lords as Gentleman Usher of the Black Rod, a post he held to his death. Sir Michael Biddulph was succeeded by Lieut.-General Sir Frederick Middleton, K.C.M.G., C.B., known to many previous generations of Gentlemen Cadets as Commandant of the Royal Military College, Sandhurst. The last appointment made by Queen Victoria was that gallant old soldier, General Sir Hugh Gough, one of the great soldier family of Goughs, who had won the Victoria Cross as a subaltern in the Indian Mutiny with Sir Deighton Probyn, Sir John Watson, Sir Charles Gough his brother, and Sir Sam Browne.

King Edward's only appointment during his short reign was General Sir Robert Low, G.C.B., who ended a long and distinguished career as a soldier by the remarkable military achievement known as the Relief of Chitral, certainly one of the most complete strategical and tactical successes recorded amongst our smaller wars.

The office has twice fallen vacant during the present King's reign. His Majesty's first selection, when Sir Robert Low died, was General Sir Arthur Wynne, G.C.B., who had distinguished himself in many a war from the Jowaki Expedition of 1877 and the Afghan War which immediately followed it, down to the South African War of 1899–1901. Sir Arthur retired from the office of Keeper of the Jewel House after five years, and was succeeded by the present holder.[1]

[1] See Appendix A for list of Keepers from 1042–1920.

CHAPTER IX

POMP AND CIRCUMSTANCE

The salary of the Keeper £50—His perquisites—Rooms in all the
King's houses—And at the Tower of London—His table
provided from the King's kitchen—Beer, wine, and spirits as
seemed good to him—The King's New Year gift money—
Presents from the Ambassadors—Perquisites and privileges—
How they were encroached upon—How the King decided—
The King and Sergeant Painter—The Court Jeweller's fee—
A breeze with the Queen's Household—The Keeper and the
Crown—The Keeper a Privy Councillor—His official robes—
" He hath no superior officer "—Pilfering of the Royal Jewels—
The office worth £10,000 a year—The Keeper's modest salary
now—But no fear of the block on Tower Hill.

IN ancient days in England the salaries of
dignitaries and holders of offices under the
Crown were comparatively small, but the
emoluments direct and indirect were often
very valuable. Thus the official salary of the Keeper
of Jewel House was, up to Tudor and Stuart days,
only £50 a year, paid annually in arrears. But since it
is manifest that no one could live, however economic-
ally, and keep up his position on this nebulous
income the kings of those days allowed, what we
now think vulgar, that is perquisites. Three hundred
years hence, perchance butlers and hall-porters will
be as much above the region of subsidiary salaries

as is now the Lord Chancellor or the Master of the Horse, and as is, also from reliable information, the Keeper of the Jewel House. In this respect the Keeper of the King's Treasure in those days fared by no means indifferently, his salary of £50 being a mere bagatelle which might almost have been dispensed with. To start with, apartments were reserved for him in all the King's palaces, as well as at the Tower of London, for it was his duty to travel with the King wherever he went, and to take with him such articles of the Regalia and Royal plate as the King might have occasion to require. When in London the Keeper would reside in the Royal Palace, whilst his deputy was quartered at the Tower in immediate charge of the Regalia. Thus he lived rent free, though perhaps not always under the most comfortable conditions according to modern ideas, for there were a large number of similar officials in the King's retinue, and each wrangled with another as to who should have this accommodation or that, and who should have precedence in this minor matter, as in greater.

The Keeper of the Regalia not only lodged free of charge, but also was his table plenteously provided from the King's kitchen and from the King's cellar. The allotment of solid refreshment laid down sounds almost immodest, being no less than fourteen "double-dishes" per diem. What a double dish was is not quite clear, but at the Coronation of James II there is a great enumeration of the "singular dishes," and the diagram of the table shows all these dishes to be round in shape. Presumably, therefore, a double dish was oblong in shape, was twice the size, and held twice as much as a singular dish. And whereas our forefathers thought little of the light viands of these days, we may conclude that the fourteen double dishes held little but solid meats and puddings. Though appetites seem to have been large in those days, there appears to be an ample margin in this allowance for the Keeper not only to feed himself and a moderate following on a fairly liberal scale, but also to entertain his friends. Nor was the allowance of liquid refreshment less liberal; for in this respect we learn that the Keeper was allowed as much beer, wine, and spirits as seemed good unto him, and presumably to his guests.

Apart from these creature comforts more substantial benefits in hard cash accrued to the guardian of the Regalia. His Christmas box was a handsome money present which came out of the King's New Year gift money. This gift money, which usually amounted to £3000 in gold, was presented to the King by members of the nobility, each according to his quality, and the Keeper received it on behalf of His Majesty for redistribution. Out of this sum he was entitled to keep one shilling in the pound as his own share, and to make what profit he could in distributing the remainder in silver, the ratio between

I

the gold pound and its exchange into silver being a
sensible source of profit. It was calculated that this
percentage and rate brought in from £300 to £400
every New Year to the Keeper, which we must not
forget was equal in value to £3000 to £4000 at this
date.

The highest in the land in days of old were not
above taking presents, or as we should now vulgarly
call them, tips; indeed, these were a recognised
source of income. The Earl of Essex, when Keeper
of the Regalia in the reign of Henry VIII, saw
nothing derogatory in taking presents of money from
foreign ambassadors, for it was the custom that he
should do so, and it was as much an obligation on
the part of those ambassadors to gratify the Earl
of Essex as it is in our day to gratify the present
Earl of Essex's butler. The occasion used for this
gratifying exchange of courtesies was when the
Keeper carried presents from His Majesty to these
ambassadors, and these occasions must have been
frequent or else the gratifications must have been
liberal, for on an average the Keeper counted on
making another £300 a year in this way, and again
we must multiply that sum by ten to get its present
value.

We are indebted to Sir Gilbert Talbot, who was
Keeper of the Jewel House in the reign of Charles II,
for an exact account of the ancient rights and privileges of his office. These he had received from Sir

Henry Mildmay, who was Keeper in the reigns of James I and Charles I, who in his turn passed on what had been enjoyed by Thomas Cromwell, Earl of Essex, Keeper in the reign of Henry VIII.

Sir Gilbert Talbot's preamble reads :—

" The Master of the Jewel House holdeth his place by Patent, for life, under the Broad Seal of England to enjoy all the perquisites and privileges which any of his predecessors at any time enjoyed"[1]

These are as follows :—

1. A fee of £50 per annum out of the Exchequer.
2. A Table of 14 double dishes per diem.
3. £300 per annum out of the New Year's gift money.
4. The carrying of presents to Ambassadors.
5. The small presents at New Year's tide.
6. Anciently Treasurers of the Chamber which office was a branch of the Jewel House.
7. Frequently Privy Councillors, as were Cromwell and the two Cary's.
8. Right to buy, keep and present all his Majesty's Jewels (when given).
9. Choice of his under Officers.
10. Choice of the King's and Queen's Goldsmiths and Jewellers.
11. £20 in gold, upon signing of the Goldsmith's bill.

[1] From the MS. written in 1680, in possession of Mrs. Lowndes. See Appendix D.

12. Lodging in all the King's houses.
13. A close wagon (when the Court moveth) for his own goods ; and two carts for his officers.
14. Precedence in Courts and Kingdom.
15. Privilege of the Drawing room.
16. Robes at the Coronation.
17. In Procession place before all Judges.
18. He putteth on, and taketh off the King's Crown.
19. He keepeth all the Regalia.
20. He hath lodgings, etc., in the Tower.
21. A servant there to keep the Regalia.
22. He hath no superior Officer.
23. He furnisheth plate to Ambassadors and all great Officers.
24. He remandeth it when Ambassadors return ; and Officers remove or die.
25. He provideth a Garter and plain George for Knights of the Garter.

Having thus recounted his rights and privileges, Sir Gilbert Talbot in a long petition to King Charles II pointed out how these had been encroached upon through, he avers, the machinations of Hyde, the Lord Chancellor. The first great grievance was that his " 14 double dishes " per diem, which we have seen carried in their wake as much bread, beer, and wine as seemed good to the Keeper, were discontinued, and in place thereof he was given a meagre £120 per annum as board wages. This was indeed an economy for the Treasury, for the scale of board wages had formerly been fixed at 35s. per diem on such occasions as the fourteen double dishes, etc., could not on the line of march, for instance, be supplied. 35s. a day came to a matter of £641 per annum, so that the Keeper stood to lose £421 each year on the deal. Naturally this raised his wrath.

In connection with the next item of complaint, Sir Gilbert Talbot did somewhat better. His right of old was £300 out of the money presented to the King by the nobles in accordance with their patents at the New Year. The total sum thus presented was, we have seen, about £3000, so that the Keeper's percentage was liberal enough; but in addition, though the Keeper received the £3000 on behalf of the King in gold, he was allowed to disburse it to those to whom it was distributed in silver, whereby he calculated to make another shilling in the pound profit, making a total of £450. King Charles, evidently bored with details, and the persistence of Sir Gilbert, compounded for £400 yearly, and that sum became the Keeper's fixed perquisite under this head.

Then came a very knotty point. Formerly, apparently, the Keeper of the Jewel House received the equivalent of £300 per annum for " carrying presents " to the foreign ambassadors. These presents consisted of plate, and the Keeper not only carried them, but made his percentage out of the goldsmiths on their value, as well as receiving such gratuities or favours as the ambassadors might give him in return compliment. But the Duke of Buckingham having prevailed upon Charles I to make these presents in the form of jewels instead of plate, and the Keeper of the day, who was Sir Henry Mildmay, having incautiously remarked that he knew nothing about the purchase of jewels, this useful addition to his income was taken from him and given to the Lord Chamberlain, who possibly knew no more about jewels, but gladly added this item to his income.

The Keeper of the Jewel House was entitled to twenty-eight ounces of silver-gilt plate every New Year's Day as part of his emoluments. This he took either in kind or cash, as seemed good to him. Nobody seems to have interfered with this item, but the Lord Chamberlain, Lord Manchester, is in Sir Gilbert Talbot's bad books over a cognate matter. Apparently certain nobles had yearly, probably as a sort of tribute for their patents, to make small presents of gold to the King on New Year's Day. These can have consisted of little more than a few coins, for the total amount only came to £30 or £40. Each offering of gold was contained in a purse, and both the gold and the purses were handed on to the Keeper as his perquisite. Lord Manchester claimed these purses, but not the gold, as his own, as did his successor the Earl of St. Albans.

But the Keeper complained to the King, and contested this claim : so the King, who was for a pleasant life and as few worries as possible, decided that the purses by ancient right belonged to the Keeper, but that if he was a wise knight he would give five or six of them yearly to the Lord Chamberlain as a peace offering. This accordingly he did, and all parties appear to have been contented.

Anciently the Keeper of the Jewel House was also Treasurer of the Chamber, his title then being Master and Treasurer of the Jewel House. But on the Restoration, with so many faithful but needy Royalists to be provided for, the office was divided, and the Keeper felt this deeply ; for apparently the Treasury portion was the richer, indeed it became five times more valuable as a source of income than the Jewel House.

The choice and appointment of his subordinates was, and is, the right of the Keeper of the Jewel House, and the reason for this was somewhat curiously demonstrated. Apparently on one occasion a vacancy having occurred, a certain Sergeant Painter went direct to the King and asked him for the post. Charles II, with his usual good nature, at once consented. Painter armed with this authority came to the Keeper and demanded the appointment. But Sir Gilbert Talbot refused to accept him, and said he would take the King's orders himself. Going to the King, Sir Gilbert asked whether

His Majesty had appointed Sergeant Painter to the vacancy in the Jewel House. The King said he had done so. Sir Gilbert pointed out that by right all such appointments were made by the Keeper, so that he might be sure of the honesty and loyalty of those under him who were guarding the Jewels and plate. " Well," said the King, " for this time let it pass, and I will invade your right no more." Sir Gilbert then asked if the King would be security for all the Jewels and plate entrusted to Painter. To which the King replied, " No, indeed will I not; and if that be requisite I recommend him not." Having made this remonstrance to draw attention to his rights, the Keeper withdrew his objections, and calling up Sergeant Painter appointed him to the post.

One of the handsomest perquisites of the Keeper was the appointing of the Goldsmiths and Jewellers to the King and Queen. These appointments were worth £800 each to him, that being the sum paid him for this privilege by the firms appointed. During the confusion of the Restoration the Keeper nearly lost this valuable addition to his income, for a Groom of the Chambers, named Coronell (Colonel ?) Blage, annexed the right and offered the appointment to Alderman Backwell for £800. The Alderman, however, hearing that the right of appointment had heretofore belonged to the Keeper of the Jewel House, drew back and informed the Keeper. That

officer at once intervened with such emphasis that
" Mr. Blage deserted his pretensions," and the £800
went to its lawful assignee. The Keeper no longer
appoints the Court Jewellers, and nobody gets the
£800 for doing so.

The Court Jewellers and Goldsmiths, according to
ancient custom, made to the Keeper a present of £20
in gold when he signed their annual bills. This was
in the bad old days doubtless a bribe, so that the
bill might not be too closely scrutinised. We may
also be well assured that the £20 did not come out
of the Jeweller's pocket, but was fully covered by
adding a little here and there to each item in the bill.
It is refreshing to learn that as early as the seventeenth century, some Keepers recognising the ques-
tionable nature of this £20 present, refused absolutely
to take it, and checked the bills honestly. Needless
to say that at the present day the Keeper is put
into no such invidious position ; in fact he never
sees a bill, all these being discharged by the Lord
Chamberlain, who, it is hardly necessary to mention,
does not receive a £20 honorarium from Messrs.
Gerrard, the Court Jewellers, for doing so.

In the days when the Keeper of the Regalia
followed the King wherever he went, rooms were
reserved for him, his officers, and his servants, in
all the King's palaces. Then breezes, as might now,
arose amongst the various Court officials as to the
apportioning of the available accommodation. Thus

we find the Keeper recording that, in 1660, the lodgings provided for him at the Palace in Whitehall were rude, dark, and intermixed with those of the Queen's Household. The dining-room was "a kind of wild barn, without any covering beside rafters and tiles. The Keeper's lodgings were two ill chambers, above stairs, and the passage to them dark at noon-day."

Perhaps naturally under these mixed conditions, and tempers being shortened by the rain pouring through the tiles during dinner, the relations between the Keeper, who was a member of the King's Household, and the members of the Queen's Household, became colder and colder, till at length each flew to their titular heads. The Queen's Household no doubt had excellent grounds of complaint, as had also doubtless the Keeper, and thus both were even. But the Keeper, being an astute person, played a final trump card; he said he could not be responsible for the King's plate and treasure with so many people in and out who were not under his orders. It was really not safe, he said; it was absolutely essential that he should have the whole set of lodgings to himself. So out went the Queen's Household, and the Keeper and all his officers were installed in a compact and unassailable mass.

The Keeper of the Jewel House has always been, and is to this day, a member of the Sovereign's Household. In former times he held certain rights, privileges, and precedence, but these in the course of ages have mostly melted away, though his warrants of appointment have from time to time stated that he was to enjoy all the rights and privileges of his predecessors. For instance, one of the rights, or rather, as we should now style it, one of the duties of the Keeper, was never to let the crown out of his keeping. So definite were his instructions that he had personally to take the crown from the Tower to the King's Palace, and with his own hand place it on the King's head. He had then to follow the King wherever he went, say to the opening of Parliament, never allowing the crown to be out of his sight. On the return to the palace he was to take the crown off the King's head, and return with it to the Tower. This procedure is now much altered. The Keeper of the Jewel House, on demand of the Lord Chamberlain, hands over the crown to him or his representative, takes a receipt for it, and has no further responsibility till the crown is returned to him.

In Tudor days the Keeper of the Jewel House was generally made a Privy Councillor, and if not already of higher rank was created a Knight, and ranked as the senior Knight Bachelor of the Kingdom. At a coronation he wore a robe very like that of a Baron, but with a crown embroidered in gold on his left shoulder. A robe very like this is still the official robe of the Keeper; it is, however, of crimson silk more like that of a Knight Grand

Cross of the Bath, with a golden crown embroidered on the left shoulder. The whole costume may be seen in Sir George Naylor's book of the *Coronation of George IV*.

In precedence the Keeper ranked after Privy Councillors and before all Judges, and had, as at present, the private entrée at all State functions at Court. As late as the seventeenth century none below the rank of Baron, and the Keeper of the Jewel House who ranked as a Baron, were allowed this privilege.

A very curious privilege which the Keeper of the Jewel House still retains is that " he hath no superior Officer in Court or Kingdom." He receives no orders except from the King himself or conveyed to him through the Lord Chamberlain. The origin of this rule is not far to seek, for otherwise, in less settled days, anybody who was in a position to do so might have ordered the Keeper to hand over portions of the Regalia or Royal Plate. As a safeguard against the Keeper or his officers tampering with the Crown Jewels, it was open to a committee detailed by the Lords of the Treasury to inspect the Regalia at such times as they might think fit. In spite, however, of these precautions there is very conclusive evidence that the regal emblems were constantly being tampered with, valuable stones extracted and coloured glass inserted to replace them. Who committed these abstractions, whether the Keeper himself or whether by the King's command, is not certain ; perhaps more probably the losses were due to the Crown Jewels being insufficiently protected and guarded. As late as the reign of James II we have a record of the new King paying as much as £500 for the *hire* of Jewels for the day of his Coronation, presumably to replace pieces of coloured glass found in the regal emblems. A somewhat notable instance of this is the large, faceted globe or monde which used to be on the top of the King's Crown. This was always described as a very valuable aquamarine, and is portrayed on the crowns of several sovereigns. Unhappily, on examination the magnificent aquamarine was found to be of glass, the real stone having been removed in some previous reign and replaced by a worthless imitation. This glass replica, as before mentioned, is shown as a curiosity amongst the Crown Jewels.

To emphasise the position of the Keeper of the Regalia he was frequently made a Privy Councillor, and amongst those specially mentioned as such, are Thomas Cromwell, Earl of Essex, and the two Cary's, probably father and son, who succeeded each other. Taken as a whole, therefore, it is evident that the office was both in dignity and emoluments a very valuable one, and as such naturally much sought after. It is calculated that, allowing for the difference of value then and now, that about £10,000 a year would be the present equivalent of the Keeper's pay and emoluments.   Both Thomas Cromwell and Sir Henry Mildmay became very rich indeed, whilst Sir Gilbert Talbot died by no means a pauper.

Compared to this brilliant and opulent past the present may seem a less entrancing vista for the Keeper of the Jewel House; but times and customs have changed, and an old officer with £300 a year added to his pension, with snug quarters provided by the King in the Tower of London, finds himself in a more honorable and less precarious position than his ancient predecessors with their bribes and perquisites, but surrounded by jealous enemies, and always with the block on Tower Hill upon the near horizon.

CHAPTER X

THE ROMANCE OF THE GREAT GEMS

THE history of England might be written round the gems that adorn, and in many cases, grace the regal emblems. Of the greater precious stones there are connected and authentic traditions which carry them back to Edward the Confessor, or to the Black Prince, or to Queen Elizabeth ; but besides these are many thousands of smaller stones set in the crowns, some of which, as is testified by their cutting, are of untold antiquity. These have probably been set and reset in the crowns of the Kings of England for centuries, but being of no remarkable size or shape are not recognisable in the presentments of ancient crowns. Even in this year of grace it is found impossible to pictorially portray a diamond so as to give even moderate justice to the original. Leaving, therefore, the smaller stones to their silent testimony, it is possible to give the romantic stories of the greater gems.

Of these the one which claims perhaps to the British Empire the greatest interest is the great ruby, which is indeed as large as a small hen's egg, and is given the place of honour in front of the King's State Crown. This is the celebrated and historic jewel which first in its English history belonged to the Black Prince, the eldest son of Edward III.

The ruby came to him in true knightly fashion on the field of battle. In those days the potentates of Europe were accustomed to lend each other armed forces, large or small, to accomplish such military achievements as might be dear to one or the other or to both. Thus it was that Edward III lent a small force of some four or five thousand English troops to Don Pedro, King of Castille, to be employed during a short campaign in Spain. Mainly through the skill of the Black Prince, aided

THE BLACK PRINCE
WITH THE FAMOUS RUBY IN HIS CORONET

by the courage of the English soldiers, Don Pedro defeated his enemies at the Battle of Najera, which is near Vittoria, where the Duke of Wellington many centuries later won another British victory. In gratitude for this signal service Don Pedro gave to the Black Prince his most treasured jewel, an enormous ruby.

The ruby, red as human blood, had come to Don Pedro in bloody fashion. In 1367 it belonged to the King of Granada, another minor sovereign in Spain, and Don Pedro greatly coveted the greatest gem of the Western world, as it then probably was. He therefore took direct action towards obtaining the stone, and in cold blood slaughtered the King of Granada and carried off the ruby. His gift to the Black Prince, therefore, however generous it may have seemed, was not improbably a decent pretext for getting rid of a treasure ignobly acquired, and which when once possessed lost its value. How old the ruby was in 1367 history does not relate, but it bears visible evidence that it had previous to that date an oriental origin, which may have extended over many centuries.

This is judged by the fact that at the top of the ruby may be seen a piercing, made evidently so as to enable it to be worn suspended from a necklace. This piercing of precious stones is of very ancient oriental origin, from which it is concluded that the ruby came from the East, and not improbably from

K

Burmah, where similar rubies have been found. The ancient piercing has in a later century been filled up by inserting a small ruby in a gold setting.

However ancient its origin, the ruby came into the possession of the British Crown in 1367–68, and has since been through many and great adventures before it reached its present well-earned security in the Tower of London.

The Black Prince, using the pierced hole, had the ruby sewn to the velvet cap he wore under his coronet, and an ancient print shows the gem thus disposed. The Prince died in 1376, a year before his father, and therefore never came to the throne; but he bequeathed the ruby to his son, who afterwards became Richard II. Henry IV, on usurping the throne probably usurped the ruby with it, but it does not reappear in history till the next reign, that of Henry V. Here it had a very notable and thrilling adventure, for it took part in one of the greatest of British victories, the battle of Agincourt. It was the custom in those days for the King, if a doughty warrior, and Kings were expected to be so, to take the field with his troops and to fight at their head. Nor did he go to battle meanly clad, or disguised as a knight of small account. On the contrary, he went armed, caparisoned, and mounted, as a king; and so that there should be no mistake about it, wore a regal diadem round his helmet. Thus went forth Henry V on the morn of Agincourt, and glittering on the front of his coroneted helmet was the great ruby. As the battle swayed backwards and forwards many exciting encounters took place between redoubted champions on either side, each choosing out an opponent worthy of his steel. In this knightly quest the great Duc d'Alençon, searching no doubt for an English duke or earl, came upon a commanding figure, who from his bearing, rich armour, and coroneted helmet was evidently a knight of importance. Him, therefore, the Duc d'Alençon challenged to mortal combat ; and lesser folk, as was the chivalry of the day, stood aside and held the lists.

The duel was fierce and strong, and many a shrewd blow was dealt and parried, but at length Henry V prevailed, and the Duc d'Alençon was unhorsed and made a prisoner, to be later held to ransom. It was only after the battle was over, and the victory of Agincourt emblazoned for ever on the standards of England, that the King being unhelmeted, and his armour removed, it was discovered that a shrewd blow had only just missed the great ruby, or perhaps had been turned by it. Indeed, a mighty cut from the Duc d'Alençon's sword had hewn off a portion of the golden diadem in which the ruby was set.'

Some say that this was the last occasion on which the ruby has figured in battle, whilst others are of opinion that so striking a jewel would always have been in the crowns of succeeding monarchs.

If this was so another decisive battle, though not on the victorious side, may be added to its war record. A little more than a hundred years after the battle of Agincourt was fought in England another battle of importance, which decided not only a local quarrel, but influenced the course of the history of the nation. In this battle, which was fought at Bosworth Field, Richard III, the Hunchback, was defeated by Henry Tudor. According to the well-known story, when the tide of battle turned against him, Richard, who had worn his crown throughout the day, though probably behind a safe barbed wire of knights, was seized with panic, and to ensure a less conspicuous retreat, took off his crown and hid it in a hawthorn bush. There some lucky underling, doubtless in quest of loot, found it in good and appropriate season, so that the victorious army was through its appointed leaders enabled to crown there and then, amidst the dead and dying, Henry VII King of England. Let us hope that the great ruby was in the crown on this historic occasion, for it was the birth of the House of Tudor.

Henry VII was the issue of a romance nearly connected with the Black Prince, and through him with the ruby. 'When Henry V died, Katherine, his widow, having first tasted of royalty, became a mere woman, and for love of a mere man married a plain but stalwart soldier from the ranks named

Owen Tudor. It was their grandson who was the victor at Bosworth, and who was there crowned Henry VII.

The next recorded adventure of the great ruby came more than a century later, though doubtless if it could speak it would have much to say of what it saw or suffered during those hundred and sixty-four intervening years. When Charles I was beheaded, it was ordered by Parliament that all the insignia of royalty should be destroyed and the gems set therein sold to the best advantage. In the list which we have of the Regalia, which was in accordance with this order totally destroyed, defaced, or sold, we find the item : " To one large ballas ruby wraped in paper value £4." Thus humbly disguised and lowly priced the Black Prince's ruby passed to some unknown purchaser. He may have been a Royalist in disguise, or he may have been a dealer in stones, or this may have been a spurious deal to favour a Parliamentarian whom it was wished to gratify ; perchance even it passed by favour to a fair lady beloved of a Roundhead. But whatever its adventures during the Commonwealth era, we find the ruby safe and sound back in the State Crown of Charles II.

As is related in the account of Colonel Blood's attempt to steal the Crown,[1] for convenience of porterage the arches were battered in and the

[1] See p. 183.

rim bent double, so that it might conveniently be slipped into a bag carried for the purpose. During this rough treatment many of the stones fell out, and amongst others the great ruby, which, when the marauders were captured, was found in Parrett's pocket. That this large ballas ruby, as it is described, was the Black Prince's ruby is very clearly evident, because the setting of Charles II's State Crown is still in existence, in which may be seen a vacant hole the exact size and shape of the Black Prince's ruby. Curiously enough, this historic setting is not State property, but passed into private possession, and was last owned by the late Lord Amherst of Hackney.

The ruby is not set clear, but has a gold backing, how ancient is not known, but so old that no jeweller will run the risk of taking it off to weigh and accurately measure the stone. Messrs. Rundell and Bridge more than a century ago refused to do so, and Messrs. Garrard, the Court Jewellers, at this day would be equally diffident. A stone so old as this, though apparently perfectly sound, is not wisely put to so severe a strain as might be occasioned in removing the gold setting.

That was the latest great adventure which is recorded of the ruby. From that time to this, a stretch of two and a half centuries, it has passed in succession to thirteen Kings and Queens of England, and now occupies the pride of place in front of the

State Crown of King George V, and rests secure and safe in the Tower of London.

More famous even than the Black Prince's ruby, and with perhaps an even more exciting history, is the great diamond known throughout the world by the name given to it many centuries ago in the East, Koh-i-Nur, or Mountain of Light. This priceless jewel was found in the diamond-fields of Golconda in Southern India, and is first heard of when in the possession of the King of Golconda. The King of Golconda was a petty chieftain much too insignificant to own so great a stone, the fame of which had spread throughout India, and stretched its alluring light so far north as the throne of the Great Mogul at Delhi. The Great Mogul at this time was the Emperor Shah Jehan, and as Golconda was some 1500 miles from Delhi, the ordinary procedure of sending an army to knock Golconda on the head and seize the jewel was not feasible. Shah Jehan, therefore, employed such guile and diplomacy as is dear to the Oriental heart to obtain his desire in a less expensive manner. Thus by bribery and cajolery the jewel passed, and quite fittingly from a historic point of view, into the hands of a great monarch.

The Koh-i-Nur is first recorded as having been seen by a European in 1665, when the French traveller Tavernier was shown it, then in the

possession of the Emperor Aurungzebe at Delhi.
With the Great Moguls it remained till 1739, when it
started on the more adventurous and tragic period
of its career.

In that year the great invasion from the West,
under Nadir Shah, King of Persia, swept through
the Punjab and laid Delhi and the unworthy successor of great Kings at his feet. Mahomed Shah
was the unworthy successor, and having lost his
kingdom, thought that at any rate he would cling
to the Koh-i-Nur, thereby to provide himself
with food and sustenance for the remaining years
of his life. To Nadir Shah the existence of the great
stone was well known; indeed it was to be one of the
great prizes of the war, but search where they
would, neither he nor his army of followers could
find the diamond. Where searchings and direct
action failed, a little judicious love-making succeeded. Amongst Mahomed Shah's large assortment
of wives was one who was not impervious to the
gallant attacks of one of the bright knights of the
conquering hosts. In the intervals of talking about
more engrossing subjects during their midnight
meetings, this frail, comparatively fair, but undoubtedly indiscreet damsel, divulged the great
secret.

From personal observation she declared, and who
should know better than a lady who occasionally
shared his couch and his affections, the Emperor

Mahomed Shah kept the Koh-i-Nur day and night concealed in the folds of his turban. The bright but dusky knight immediately communicated this interesting piece of information to Nadir Shah. That potentate, instead of taking the commoner course of murdering the wearer of this valuable turban, or at the least committing burglary with violence, chose a more courteous but equally effective means of gaining possession of the diamond. He gave orders that a banquet should be prepared, and as the guest of honour invited Mahomed Shah. Again Nadir Shah did not mix ground glass with his guest's food, nor did he poison his wine : two obvious methods ; nor did he make him drunk and then steal the jewel. Neither was the gorgeous menial who waved a fan behind the royal diners instructed to thrust a dagger between the shoulder-blades of Mahomed Shah. The acquisition was much more diplomatically achieved.

In the East if one prince or potentate, or even a person of lower degree, wishes to pay a marked compliment to another, he after extolling the extreme elegance and richness of the other's turban, whilst deprecating the value of his own, proposes as a mark of friendship and regard that they shall exchange turbans. In the more sordid West there might be some economic souls who would not wear their best head-gear when such interchanges of courtesies were imminent, but in the East the turban is a social insignia, and the higher a person's degree the more magnificent his turban. Consequently, when two kings meet each other at dinner or other State occasions, it may safely be conjectured that they will wear their most magnificent turbans, each trusting that his own will outvie that of the other. Even an exchange which might entail a sensible loss would not be without its compensations, for all the courtiers on the other side would extol the magnificence and richness of the late possessor.

Mahomed Shah very naturally did not for a moment foresee that so great a compliment would be paid him by the conqueror, or he would assuredly have left the Koh-i-Nur at home that night. To his horror and surprise, during the course of the dinner Nadir Shah made him a most polite speech, extolled his valour and wisdom, swore eternal friendship, and as a sign and token of the same suggested that they should exchange turbans! To the luckless Mahomed Shah no course was open but to accept the compliment with the best grace he could muster. It is not surprising to learn that during the rest of the feast Nadir Shah was in excellent spirits, whilst Mahomed Shah appears to have lost his appetite.

Thus passed the great diamond to the King of Persia, who when he returned to his own land, took it with him. But it brought him no good fortune, for he was in due course murdered, and the

Koh-i-Nur was taken by one of his bodyguard, an Afghan named Ahmed Shah. This soldier of fortune escaped to Afghanistan . with the diamond, and there eventually became Amir or King of that country and founder of the Durani dynasty. In 1772 Ahmed Shad died and was succeeded by his son Taimur Shah, to whom also passed the Koh-i-Nur. Shah Suja, the next occupant of the throne at Kabul, succeeded also to the possession of the famous diamond, but it brought him no good fortune, for he was deposed and fled for his life to Lahore, taking the stone with him. There he found asylum with the Maharajah Runjeet Singh, the Lion of the Punjab, but as he soon found, only on condition that he handed over the Koh-i-Nur to his host.

In Lahore the celebrated stone was seen by Lord Auckland's sister, the Hon. Emily Eden, in 1838-39. Ten years later the threatening attitude of the Sikhs, combined with repeated and overt acts of hostility, compelled the East India Company to settle once and for all with this turbulent neighbour. With slender forces Lord Gough advanced to subjugate the Sikhs, and in the three great and hard-fought battles of the Sutlej, Goojerât, and Chillianwalla, laid in the dust the vaunted power of this military race. The Punjab was annexed to the territories administered by the East India Company, the Maharajah Runjeet Singh ceased to reign, and the Koh-i-Nur passed to the British Army as part of the spoils of war.

During the transition stage the Punjab was administered by a board of five British officers, amongst whom were the brothers Sir John [1] and Sir Henry Lawrence. At one of the meetings of the Board the question was raised as to what was to be done with the treasure taken, amongst which was the Koh-i-Nur, there lying on the table. The Board decided to ascertain the wishes of the Directors of the East India Company, and asked Sir John Lawrence meanwhile to take charge of it. Sir John, who had many and great matters on his mind, beside which a diamond was of small import, wrapped the stone up in a piece of paper, put it into his pocket, and forgot all about it !

About six weeks after, at another meeting of the Board, a letter was read from the Governor-General, in which it was stated that it had been decided that the Koh-i-Nur should be presented by the Army of the Punjab to Queen Victoria. Sir John Lawrence listened to this pronouncement without much interest, till one of the Board mentioned incidentally that the diamond was in Sir John's safe custody !

Sir John, not being an emotional man, never turned a hair, but after hearing the debate through mounted his horse and galloped off to his bungalow. There he summoned his bearer, or valet, and

[1] Afterwards Lord Lawrence and Viceroy of India.

said : " About six weeks ago I brought home in my pocket a piece of glass wrapped in a bit of paper. What did you do with it ? "

" Cherisher of the poor, I placed that piece of glass wrapped in paper on the top of your honour's office box, and "—opening the box—" here it is ! " Being an unemotional person Sir John did not fall on his servant's neck and shed tears of gratitude ; on the contrary, he merely said, " Very good," put the diamond again in his pocket and rode off to deposit it with someone who had nothing else to think about, and a guard of soldiers to help him do so.

From Lahore to England the Koh-i-Nur was sent under special precautions in charge of Major Macheson, and on arrival was presented to Queen Victoria as a loyal tribute from the Army which had by its gallant deeds added the Punjab to the Empire.

It was on view to the public at the Great Exhibition of 1851, and when that was closed returned to the safe keeping of Queen Victoria. The size and weight of the Koh-i-Nur when first found is not accurately known, but it is conjectured that after its first cutting it weighed about 1000 carats. It is, however, known that when in the possession of Shah Jehan it had, by unskilful cutting, been reduced to 800 carats. By the orders of that Emperor an endeavour was made to get a better result, the further cutting being entrusted to a Venetian named Ortensio Borgio. His effort was not deemed satisfactory, and Borgio was fined £1000, and may be considered lucky not to have lost his head as well. When presented to Queen Victoria the diamond weighed only 186½ carats. Under the superintendence of the Prince Consort it was again cut by Coster of Amsterdam into the form of a regular brilliant. By this last cutting the stone was reduced to 106½ carats, but curiously enough looks larger and is superficially larger than it was before. This result was achieved by cutting transversely the original cone-shaped stone, this diameter being greater than the base. Queen Victoria wore the Koh-i-Nur set as a brooch, but it is now perhaps more appropriately placed in front of the State Crown of Queen Mary. The diamond can, however, be removed at pleasure and worn as a brooch.

It might be thought that so historic a stone should be set in the King's Crown, but a curious tradition regarding it is thus upheld. From very ancient days, and no doubt due to its bloody history, the Koh-i-Nur is supposed to bring misfortune to any man who may wear it, but that it brings no harm to a woman. Certainly it has brought no harm to Queen Victoria, Queen Alexandra, or Queen Mary, all of whom have worn it constantly.

When presented to Queen Victoria the Koh-i-Nur was valued at £140,000, but indeed such stones as this are from their historic association practically

THE DUKE OF WELLINGTON ASSISTING AT THE FIRST CUTTING OF THE
KOH-I-NUR

priceless. The Koh-i-Nur cannot be bought with money, and he who wishes to take it by force must first defeat the British Empire.

One of the oldest as well as one of the most valuable gems in the Jewel House is the sapphire which belonged to Edward the Confessor, and was worn by him in his Coronation ring. It would thus be considerably older than the Tower of London itself, for the Confessor came to the throne many years before the Conqueror landed in England and built the Tower. As was not an unusual custom, the ring with the sapphire was buried with Edward the Confessor probably on his finger, in his shrine at Westminster, but in the year 1101 the shrine was broken open and this and other jewels taken out.

This was the ring which appears in the legend regarding Edward the Confessor and St. John the Evangelist. According to this legend St. John on one occasion appeared before the King in the guise of a pilgrim. To him the King of his bounty gave the ring off his finger. Some little time after the ring was returned to the King with a message informing him privily of the exact day of his death. Doubtless St. John meant this for a kindly warning, so that the King might be absolutely at the height of his holiness when the call came. Most people, however, would have heartily cursed St. John for his officiousness, for few care to live with a guillotine hanging over their heads and a clock facing them ticking off the hours and minutes.

The stone has manifestly been recut, for it is at present a " rose," and that form of cutting was unknown in ancient days. Probably this was done in the reign of Charles II. It is a remarkably beautiful gem, of good colour and without flaw, and is intrinsically worth a very high sum. In the days of Edward the Confessor it was reputed to have the miraculous power of curing what was known collectively as the cramp, that is rheumatism, sciatica, and the like, but we have not heard of any later monarch testing its efficiency. The sapphire is now set in the centre of cross paté on top of the King's State Crown.

In the band at the back of the King's State Crown may be seen a very large sapphire, known as the Stuart sapphire, which has seen many adventures. What its early history was is not known, but at one end is drilled a longitudinal hole evidently made for some attachment so that the stone might be worn as a pendant. It first came into recognition in the reign of Charles II, who wore it in his crown, but whether he received it from Charles I or acquired it in his wanderings is not quite clear. At his death the sapphire passed to James II, who when he was dethroned and fled to France took it with him. James II left the sapphire to his son,

Charles Edward, the Old Pretender, who in his turn left it to his son, Henry Bentinck, known as Cardinal Yorke, by whom it was bequeathed, with other Stuart relics, to George III. George IV and William IV in turn owned it, and then it came to Queen Victoria, who very greatly prized it and had it set in the band of her State Crown, in the front and just below the Black Prince's ruby. This pride of place the Stuart sapphire resigned in favour of the Star of Africa, a portion of which Edward VII placed in the crown, symbolising the entry of the Union of South Africa into the brotherhood of the British Empire.

The Stuart sapphire is of great size, being about $1\frac{1}{2}$ inches in length by 1 in. in breadth, and is oval in shape. It is without serious flaw and of good colour, though paler than some of the best sapphires to be found in other portions of the regalia. The stone is set in a gold brooch, and can be removed and worn as a personal ornament.

As gems the two greater portions of the Star of Africa eclipse in size and brilliancy all others in the Jewel House. Though the stone may have taken a million years to form in the womb of mother earth, it only saw the light of day in 1904. In the rough when found it measured 4 in. in length, $2\frac{1}{4}$ in. in width, and $2\frac{1}{2}$ in. in depth, and weighed roughly $1\frac{1}{2}$ lb. But even this huge

L

block, as large as half a Roman brick, it was concluded was only a part of some even more gigantic diamond, for its base was clean cut as with a knife, showing that a portion perhaps as large, perhaps even larger, in some remote age, by a great convulsion of nature, had been split off. For fourteen years diligent search was made for the missing portion, for any block or spadeful of blue rock might contain it. Yet strangely enough, when by chance it was found, it came to an untimely end. A telegram from Johannesburg, dated October 18th, 1919, made this brief announcement: "A large diamond has been found on the Premier Mine. It is estimated to have weighed 1500 carats, but unfortunately had been crushed by the crusher. It is believed to be part of the other half of the Cullinan diamond."

The diamond was first known as the "Cullinan Diamond," Mr. T. M. Cullinan being at the time manager of the Premier Mine, near Pretoria, where it was found, and it is still very generally known by its first name. It was insured for the sum of £1,500,000. The Union Government of South Africa eventually became the purchasers, inspired with the happy sentiment that this magnificent diamond would be a graceful emblem of the entry of South Africa into the British Empire.

When this monster stone was presented to Edward VII it looked like a block of rock salt, as may be judged from the exact model of it now to be seen in the Jewel House. When the experts were called in they declared that it was impossible to cut a stone of this size and shape into one brilliant; they therefore recommended that following the natural cleavages it should be broken up into four parts, two of which would be very great brilliants, and two of lesser size. King Edward following this advice, and with the full consent of the donors, called in the celebrated diamond-cutters of Amsterdam, the Messrs. Coster, and put the work in hand. One can imagine the enormous anxiety and the extraordinary coolness, steadiness of hand, and skill of the man who with one tremor of the mallet or chisel might mar the greatest stone of all ages. The chisel and the steel mallet with which this delicate operation was performed are preserved at the Tower, and it is noticeable that there are only two or three dents in the chisel, showing how true and clean the strokes must have been.

Thus split up, the largest portion was cut into a pear-shaped brilliant, and set at the head of the King's Sceptre. The next largest portion was cut into a cushion-shaped brilliant, and placed in the band of the King's State Crown, just below the Black Prince's ruby. Both of these brilliants are larger and finer stones than any others, including the Koh-i-Nur. The two remaining large portions are set, one in the band, and the other in the cross

paté of Queen Mary's Crown. It may be of interest
to record the exact weight and sizes of these four
great brilliants which collectively are called the
Stars of South Africa. The largest portion, that in
the King's Sceptre, weighs 516½ carats, and measures
2⅜ in. in length and 1⅜ in. at its broadest part.
The next largest portion, that in the band of the
King's State Crown, weighs 309⅟₁₆ carats, and
measures 1⅜ in. in length, and 1⅓ inches in breadth.
The third portion, that in the band of Queen Mary's
Crown, weighs 96 carats, and the fourth portion,
which is drop shaped and is in the cross paté on the
top of Queen Mary's Crown, weighs 64 carats.
Thus it will be noticed that a rough stone weighing
3025 carats cuts down into four brilliants weighing
in the aggregate under 986 carats.

The question is often asked : " What is the value
of the Stars of South Africa ? " And it is a very
difficult one to answer, for curiously enough stones
above a certain size lose their commercial value,
for few have the money or inclination to buy gems
of enormous size, and fewer still would be bold
enough to wear them. Nobody but a King or a
Queen, for instance, could wear a diamond which on
an ordinary person would look and certainly be taken
for the lustre from a candelabra. Thus the market
becomes strictly limited, as was definitely brought
home to the owners of the Premier Mine. It was
thus that the Union Government were enabled to

buy a stone valued at £1,500,000 for £150,000, a stone which even when split into four is still of an aggregate value difficult to compute. Let us elude the difficulty and say they are worth a million and a half, and leave it at that.

It is interesting to compare the Cullinan with other well-known diamonds of size and historic value, though curiously enough even the present existence of these stones is not in all cases certain. Those, for instance, which formed part of the regalia of the late Tsar of Russia are for very obvious reasons at present in hiding. The largest of these is the Orloff, which weighs 194 carats. This great stone came from India, and was reputed to be a cleavage from the still greater stone, the Koh-i-Nur. It was stolen by a French grenadier from the eye-socket of an idol in a Hindu temple. He deserted the army and sold the stone to the captain of an English merchant ship for £2000. By him it was conveyed to Holland, where a Jew named Khojeh Raphael gave £12,000 for it ; and at once resold it to Orloff for Catherine the Great for £90,000 and an annuity of £4000 ! Since that time this great stone has remained one of the Russian Crown Jewels, and when last seen was set at the head of the sceptre of the late Tsar. Where it is now or what its fate the future may perhaps reveal.

Another large diamond, named the Shah, of very curious shape, also was amongst the Russian

Crown Jewels. It is flat and rectangular in shape, with a Persian inscription engraved upon it and a groove cut round. It weighs 86 carats and was given by the Shah of Persia to the Emperor Nicholas I. The stone is an exceptionally fine one, but owing to its peculiar shape its value can only be conjectured. The Polar Star is another very fine diamond which formed part of the Russian regalia. It was bought by the Russians in London about seventy years ago, and is described as of remarkable purity and brilliancy. It weighs 40 carats, but the price paid for it and its present value is not known. Nor its whereabouts.

The Sanci diamond has a very ancient and interesting history, and has been through many adventures. It is first heard of as belonging to Charles the Bold of Burgundy on the day he was disastrously defeated by the Swiss at the battle of Granson. According to tradition a Swiss soldier picked it up, and having no value for a piece of glass, sold it for a florin or the price of a drink. Eventually it found its way to Constantinople, and was there bought by the French Ambassador in 1570, and became henceforth known as the Great Sanci diamond. Henry III and Henry IV, both of France, were the next possessors, and whilst owned by the latter King it had a curious adventure. One of the King's followers, who had charge of the diamond, was attacked by robbers, and the faithful fellow, to save his master's treasure, swallowed it. The robbers after a stiff fight slew the servant, and not finding the stone pulled the corpse into the thicket and left it. In due course of nature, when decomposition had done its work, the brilliant was found again and was restored to the French King. The Sanci then, by sale or gift, passed into the possession of Queen Elizabeth, and remained one of the Crown Jewels of England through several reigns, and escaped the depredations of the Commonwealth. In 1669 it was still in the possession of Henrietta Maria, widow of Charles I, and was by her entrusted to the Earl of Somerset, who handed it over to James II. When that monarch fled to France he took the Sanci with him and sold it to Lousi XIV for £25,000. It long remained amongst the French Crown Jewels, and in 1791 was valued at £40,000. In the year 1835 the diamond passed to Russia, being purchased by Prince Demidoff for £75,000. Then in 1865 the Sanci returned to India, whence it probably originally came, being sold by the Demidoffs to Sir Jamsetjee Jeejeebhoy, a rich Parsee of Bombay. From him it was bought by the Maharajah of Patiala, at what price is not known, and is still in that prince's possession, and may be seen on the front of his turban on State occasions.

The Great Moghul originally weighed 787 carats, but when seen in the treasury of the Emperor Aurungzebe in 1665 by Tavernier it had been cut down to an estimated weight of 280 carats. It appears to have been given to the Emperor Shah Jehan by the Amir Jumba. It is by some supposed to be a portion cleaved off the Koh-i-Nur by some great convulsion of nature in remote ages long before either were discovered. The diamond is believed to be at present in the possession of the Shah of Persia.

The Regent or Pitt diamond was found either in Borneo or India, and weighed then 410 carats. It was bought by Mr. Pitt, Governor of Madras, for £20,400, and was subsequently sold in 1717 to the Duc d'Orleans, Regent of France, for £80,000. In the process of cutting the diamond was reduced to 136¾ carats, and was amongst the French Crown Jewels stolen during the Revolution. Later it was recovered, and is still believed to be in France.

The Hope diamond is a beautiful blue brilliant weighing 44¼ carats, and is one of those stones which is reputed to bring bad luck to its owner. It formed part of the collection of Mr. H. T. Hope, who bought it for £18,000, and after whom it is named. The stone was last heard of in the possession of an American, and quite recently the newspapers gave an account of a small child being killed in a street accident, the child being the only son of the owner of the Hope diamond.

Pearls are not like diamonds or other hard stones, which, having gone through periods of thousands of years under enormous pressure deep down in the earth, can now last for thousands more with undiminished lustre set in a ring or a crown, exposed to the free air of this terrestrial globe. The pearl is really only a sort of disease, or perhaps to put it more mildly a distemper, or milder still a pastime, on the part of the pearl oyster. A large pearl naturally takes many years to form inside the oyster's shell, whilst small ones take so many years less. Even in one or two years a foreign substance, say a small shot, will, if placed in a pearl oyster, become to all appearance a pearl of high price. Even minute effigies of elephants and Bhuddhas when introduced will, in the course of a few months, be thinly but completely coated with pearl lustre. The true and valuable pearl also had a nucleus, probably a grain of sand, and this year after year has been covered with thin coatings of pearl lustre, so that small or large it is practically solid, so solid that it cannot be broken if trodden upon. But even so it is merely the product of decades, and has not the lasting-power of diamonds, or rubies, or sapphires, or emeralds.

A marked example of the comparatively short life of pearls is furnished by a very celebrated one known as the Pearl of Portugal. This pearl was as large as a pigeon's egg ·and of that shape, and naturally at its zenith was of enormous value. Seen a few years ago by an expert, he described it as having deteriorated into nothing more valuable than a piece of chalk of the same size and shape. Owners of valuable pearls will immediately exclaim: "Oh! but that is because it was not constantly worn next the skin." There are hundreds, perhaps thousands, of women who religiously wear their pearls next their skins all day, and some even at night, under the impression that they are so preserved. One of the highest experts in pearls and precious stones, however, puts this custom on a much lower plane. He says that the wearing of pearls next the skin is no doubt good as a burnisher, likening, from a purely commercial point of view, a woman's skin to a finer form of chamois leather. But as to any preservative quality in the contact he will have none of it.

Queen Elizabeth's earrings, the four great pearls which hang beneath the arch in the King's State Crown, are, therefore, apart from their personal connection, of considerable interest, as regards the life of a pearl as a gem of value. These pearls have probably never been worn next the skin, even of a Queen. They are drop-shaped and manifestly only suitable for earrings or pendants. Yet though Queen Elizabeth died more than three hundred years ago they are still in good preservation. Thus they may remain for several centuries more if, as at present, they are kept in a perfectly air-tight compartment at an even temperature. But at best they can never outlive a diamond.

The exact history of these pearls is difficult to follow, and it is more by tradition and indirect evidence that it is assumed that they came from Queen Elizabeth. That great lady was, as all her pictures show, fond of pearls. She was a great Sea Queen, and we may be assured that her captains who quartered the globe brought home any great pearl they came across from distant seas or lands, knowing it would find a Royal purchaser. James I probably had not much use for pearls, except to horde them, but they seem not to have been amongst the Crown Jewels which he succeeded to, for they are not mentioned in the careful list that monarch made out in his own handwriting, and signed both at head and foot. This is understandable, for the pearls were Queen Elizabeth's private property to bequeath to whom she pleased. It is not clear whether Charles I ever had these pearls, but the suggestion is that he had, and that he disposed of them to meet his necessities in his wars against Cromwell. Into whose hands they fell is a matter for conjecture as well as how they passed through the next century, for the next portrayal that we come across of them is in the State Crown of another great Queen, Victoria.

They hung as pendants beneath the cross of the

arches of the crown, one at each corner. Here they were retained by Edward VII, and still occupy the same position in the State Crown of George V.

What wonderful stories those pearls could tell! Of the Great Armada and the pride of that great victory; of the bloody days of Charles I, and of his tragic death outside the window at Whitehall; of the gay days of Charles II, and the long and prosperous reign of Queen Victoria. But in all those centuries they probably had no greater adventures or dangers than they experienced together with the other Crown Jewels during the Great War of 1914–19.

The safe place in the Tower chosen for them by Edward VII is burglar-proof, fireproof, and proof against alarms and excursions; but when William the Conqueror built the Tower, he had undoubtedly never expected that it might be subject to an attack from the air. Even so he had made his roofs so thick and strong that a dropping cannon-ball might well be rebuffed. The pearls and their comrades the gems therefore looked on with calm toleration whilst the Germans waged and raged for four years over them. Indeed, they had got quite accustomed to this aerial bombardment, for though bombs fell close around them, still a miss is as good as a mile. It was only just towards the end of the war that news came which made the soldiers think that larger and heavier and more destructive bombs were likely to be used by the Germans. Then William the Conqueror, walking in the pleasant fields of heaven, said to Queen Elizabeth : "I am sorry, but I am afraid my walls and roofs cannot keep these out. You had better send your pearls away to one of the other palaces of the King, out in the open country." So the pearls and their consorts one day without any fuss just slipped off and went to stay at Windsor till the war was over. That William the Conqueror and Queen Elizabeth were wise in their decision was obvious, for leaning over the ramparts of heaven they saw one great bomb fall into the Tower moat on the west, another they saw hit the railings on the edge of the moat to the north, whilst a third hit the Mint across the road to the east, and a fourth dropped within a few yards of the Jewel House into the river to the south. The next might have sent several million pounds' worth of jewels to God knows where.

CHAPTER XI

THE CRIME OF COLONEL BLOOD

The Merry England of Charles II—An old man the sole custodian
of the Crown Jewels—The Jewels in the Martin Tower—Colonel
Blood's plans—His disguise as a parson—Mrs. Blood is seized
with " a qualme upon her stomack "—Parson Blood's gratitude
and present of gloves—A match arranged with old Edward's
daughter—The pious parson at dinner—Blood removes the
pistols—An early call—The lovers to meet—Mr. Edwards
stunned, gagged, and bound—The Crown bashed in and placed
in a bag—The Orb and Sceptre—A surprise arrival from Flanders—In hot pursuit—The Captain of the Guard nearly killed
in error—The burglars fight their way out—Reach the Iron
Gate where horses awaited them—Captured—The Crown saved
—King Charles rewards Colonel Blood.

THE Crown Jewels have been through many
vicissitudes, and have chanced across many
adventures. They have been in the midst
of the fiercest and most historic battles,
and they have lain inglorious in the shop of the
pawnbroker. But only once have they been
burglariously removed, and that in the open day,
and from the midst of the strongest fortress in
England.

This happened in the jovial reign of Charles II
when, led by a prince who drank the wine of life
to the full, the people of England were out to live

COLONEL BLOOD WHO ATTEMPTED TO STEAL THE CROWN AND ORB
IN THE REIGN OF CHARLES II
(From the National Portrait Gallery)

the free and joyous life, after the horrors of civil war and the equally distasteful restraints of the Cromwellian era. England was Merry England again, and black shadows were put right behind the eastern horizon. Officials, even those the most responsible, caught the happy vein, and drowned the dismal past in flowing bowls of rich red wine. Amidst all this joyful living, who cared to be reminded of the chains on body and soul and conscience of the prim pernicious Puritans ? That anybody would dream of attempting to steal the Crown of the beloved sovereign never occurred to the most imaginative visionary. It might be left all day and all night unguarded on the steps of St. Paul's, and no one would touch it. In the Tower of London it was surely safe enough, without throwing extra guard duties on the garrison to supply even a single sentry. Such was the spirit and the general feeling in the air, which left the Crown Jewels in sole custody of one old man, whose age was well past the allotted span.

In former reigns, as we have seen, the Jewels were stored in some strong building closely guarded, but they were now placed only in a kind of recess in the wall with a wired front opening on hinges, situated in the basement floor of the Martin Tower. The chamber where the Jewels were had only one door, but no sentry was placed on this door. In the storeys above lived Talbot Edwards, the

Assistant-Keeper of the Regalia, with his family. Talbot Edwards was then in his seventy-seventh year, as is testified by his tombstone, now let into the south wall of the Chapel of St. Peter ad Vincula, within the Tower, which records that he died three years later on September 30th, 1674, aged 80 years.

To a professional burglar, who after all only uses common sense, it would have appeared that the Crown Jewels lay in the Martin Tower simply asking to be taken by the first person enterprising enough to make the attempt. True, though the inner casket was weak, the outer safeguards were by tradition and superstition inviolable. Massive walls, a deep moat, and a battalion of the King's Guards seemed to offer an impenetrable barrier to the escape of a prisoner, or of a burglar laden with spoil. Colonel Blood was no professional burglar, but he had learnt as a soldier of fortune to be resourceful, quick to seize an opportunity, and bold in the execution of a project, however seemingly impossible. His previous experiences, and also his observations in the Tower showed him that, besides the garrison numerous civilians, men and women, lived in the fortress, and came and went when known by sight to the guards with little hindrance ; whilst known friends of those residing within might pass with almost equal freedom.

Amongst those who might expect perhaps easier

passage in and out than others would be a parson,
especially if he was on visiting terms with one of the
officials quartered in the Tower. This plain fact
commended itself to Colonel Blood, and he made his
plans accordingly. With the aid of the Mr. Clarkson
and Mr. Nathan of those days the soldier of fortune
became an everyday-looking parson, and as such
struck up a family friendship with old Talbot
Edwards.

Talbot Edwards, though Assistant-Keeper on a
fixed salary, had failed for years to draw this salary
from an impoverished Exchequer. When this was
represented to King Charles by Sir Gilbert Talbot,
that happy-go-lucky monarch remarked that if
there was no money in the Exchequer naturally
Talbot Edwards could get nothing out of it, but, he
added, the old man might exhibit the Crown Jewels
to the public, charging them such fees as he thought
that each visitor might be inclined to pay. Amongst
this paying public came Parson Blood, accompanied
by a respectable-looking female who passed as Mrs.
Blood. But just going in and looking at the Jewels,
and paying a fee, would not further Blood's designs.
He would be on no more intimate terms with the
Assistant-Keeper than hundreds of others; moreover,
there would be no reasonable excuse for coming a
second time to see the Crown Jewels. This being so,
the temporary Mrs. Blood whilst viewing the Jewels
had the misfortune to be suddenly seized with

M

" a qualme upon her stomack," and in faint tones
called upon the distressed Mr. Edwards for some
spirits. This the old man hastily procured, and the
invalid found herself so far recovered as to be able
to go upstairs and lie down for further recuperation
on Mrs. Edward's bed.

Having recovered both from the qualme and the
potency of the spirits, the loving couple departed,
profusely thanking their kind hosts. Having thus
paved the way, Parson Blood came again three
or four days later bringing four pair of white
gloves—a very handsome present in those days,
and indeed in these—from the temporary Mrs. Blood
to the permanent Mrs. Edwards. With the gloves
came overflowing messages of gratitude which
Blood delivered. Indeed, so grateful was he that
he made repeated visits to renew his protestations.
Blood thus became a familiar figure in the Tower,
and a well-known and honoured visitor of the
Assistant-Keeper.

When, however, this theme of eternal gratitude
was in danger of becoming tiresome, Blood conceived a new device for continuing and accentuating
the friendship. Apparently the temporary Mrs.
Blood had spent her nights and days in trying to
devise some means for requiting Mr. and Mrs.
Edwards for the potent and healing draught supplied
by them, as well as for the heavenly slumber as
a result enjoyed on their connubial couch. After

severe and constant wrestling with the spirit, this worthy lady had now come to the conclusion that as Mr. Edwards had " a pretty gentlewoman to his daughter," whilst she herself had (an entirely imaginary) nephew with a fortune of two or three hundred a year, a match might well be arranged between the two.

Both Mr. and Mrs. Edwards thought this an exceedingly good plan, and Miss Edwards like a good girl had not the least doubt about it. Parson Blood was therefore asked to dinner so that the project might be more fully discussed. At this meal he impressed his hosts by the piety and devotion with which he said grace, though to more critical souls it may have seemed strange that in addition to the usual benedictions he wandered off into long prayers for the King, the Queen, and all the Royal Family.

But with all this by-play Blood did not lose sight of the main object in view, which was to purloin the Crown Jewels. Therefore in the room upstairs, noticing a handsome pair of pistols on the wall, he concluded that it would be just as well if these were out of the way on the auspicious day. Thereupon promptly inventing a young Lord to whom he was most anxious to present exactly such a handsome case of pistols as these, he purchased them off Mr. Edwards and carried them away. On leaving he blessed the company in the best canonical manner, and fixed a day and hour on which he was to bring the opulent but fictitous nephew to be introduced to his future wife.

The day fixed was May 9th, 1671, and the hour 7 a.m. This was a very suitable hour for Blood's real purpose, but why Mr. Edwards and still less his daughter should consent to so untimely an hour for the first meeting of two lovers is not quite clear. On the destined day, therefore, and at the time arranged, a clerical gentleman accompanied by three friends made their way into the Tower, and passing under the Bloody Tower left the White Tower on their right, and crossing the parade ground knocked at the door of the Martin Tower. Had the guard suspected and searched these early visitors they would have found a rapier blade in each walking-stick, a dagger in each belt, and a couple of pistols in the pockets of each.

Old Mr. Edwards was up and ready to receive his guests and met them at the door, but Miss Edwards esteemed it more modest to remain in the upper regions till the impatient lover demanded her descent. She, however, sent down her maid to take stock of the gallant and to bring her up news of his general appearance and bearing. Blood with two of his companions entered with Mr. Edwards, leaving the third on some excuse or other as a look-out at the door. The look-out man, being the youngest and comeliest of the band, was at once conceived by the maid to be the suitor, and having

COLONEL BLOOD STEALING THE CROWN AND ORB

cast a brief but critical eye on him she dashed upstairs to tell her mistress what a fine fellow he was.

Whilst awaiting the appearance of the ladies
Blood suggested to Edwards that he might fill the
interval by showing his friends the Crown Jewels.
The old man readily consented, and unlocking
the door of the treasure chamber ushered in his
guests, and then in accordance with his standing
orders locked the door behind him. This was
exactly the situation which Blood had so carefully worked up to. A locked isolated chamber,
with three able-bodied men fully armed on one
side, a feeble unarmed man nearly eighty years
old on the other, and the Crown Jewels of England
the spoil of the victor in this unequal contest.
Without wasting further time they knocked Mr.
Edwards on the head with a wooden mallet brought
for that purpose amongst others, gagged him, and
left him lying on the floor for dead. Though only
stunned Edwards pretended to be dead, but heard
or saw most of what followed.

The Jewels were in a recess in the solid
walls, having a strongly caged door in two parts
opening outwards. Inside were the two crowns,
the Crown of England and the King's State
Crown, the Sceptre and Orb, as well as several
pieces of valuable plate, including the State salt
cellar lately presented to Charles II by the City of
Exeter. Blood, who knew from his previous visits

exactly what was there, naturally had made his plans to carry off the portions of the Regalia which were at the same time the most portable and the most valuable. The Crown of England was large and heavy, and was set with stones of considerable value, but the King's State Crown was lighter and more easily compressed, and had set in its front the great and priceless ruby of the Black Prince, and was also rich with diamonds and lesser gems. Both crowns had been made for Charles II by Sir Robert Vyner, and both, it may be mentioned in passing, survive to this day, though in curiously different surroundings. The Crown of England is in the Tower of London, and the shell of Charles II's State Crown, bereft of all its precious stones, came into the possession of the late Lord Amherst of Hackney. Blood, therefore, selected the King's State Crown for his prey.

Besides the Crown there were two other regal emblems portable and set with precious stones. These were the King's Sceptre and Orb. Both are now in the Tower of London, the Orb much as it was in those days, and the Sceptre the same except that the great Star of Africa has been since introduced into its head. These three then, the State Crown, the Sceptre, and the Orb, were the settled project of the raid. Mr. Edwards having been satisfactorily disposed of, Blood seized the Crown, and using the same wooden mallet as had been used on the custodian's head, battered in the arches of the Crown and flattened in the band, that it might thus fit into a bag made for the purpose which he wore under his parson's gown. This rough treatment naturally disturbed the setting of the stones, and some of these, including the Black Prince's ruby, fell out, but were hastily gathered up and put into their pockets by the worthy trio. To the second marauder, Parrett by name, was assigned the custody of the Orb. This was quite a simple matter; he just thrust it as it was into the slack of his breeches, and dropped the folds of his cloak so as to hide the protuberance.

The third accomplice was to carry off the Sceptre, but as this could not conveniently be concealed about his person, he was provided with a file wherewith to file the Sceptre in two so that it might fit into a bag which he carried for the purpose under his cloak. He was busily engaged on this job when a most dramatic event occurred.

Old Mr. Edwards had a son who had served as a soldier in Flanders with Sir Tohn Talbot, and having landed in England, obtained leave to visit his father at the Tower. By an extraordinary coincidence he happened to arrive at this very moment, and strode at once to the Martin Tower.

Outside the door of his father's residence he found a young man standing, who asked him his business, and who he wished to see. As this was an unusual greeting to receive at the front door of one's own home, young Edwards concluded that the stranger himself was seeking an interview, and passing through said he would see if he could be received. The young man at the door, who was in fact Colonel Blood's sentry, as young Edwards went upstairs, immediately warned his confederates in the treasure chamber below, and they made haste to depart, taking the Crown and Orb, but leaving the Sceptre as it had not yet been filed in two.

Old Mr. Edwards was not bound, so that directly Colonel Blood and his accomplices fled he pulled the gag out of his mouth, and yelled with good heart and lungs, "TREASON ! MURDER !" Miss Edwards hearing these alarming shouts ran downstairs, and seeing her father wounded and the disorder in the Jewel House, rushed out on to the parade ground by the White Tower and shrieked, "TREASON ! The CROWN is stolen !" This gave the alarm to all and sundry, and amongst others to young Edwards and Captain Beckham who were still upstairs. Captain Beckham was married to one of old Mr. Edwards' daughters, and was one of the party invited to be present at the betrothal. Blood and Parrett, followed by the other two, had pushed along without suspicious haste, but on hearing the alarm raised were seen to nudge each other. However, they passed unchallenged under the Bloody Tower where was then the main guard, guarding the only gate giving egress from the inner fortress, and thence were making their way along Water Lane towards the Byward Tower.

Beyond the Byward Tower was a drawbridge, now replaced by a permanent structure, at which a yeoman stood on duty, and to him the pursuers shouted to stop the clerical party ahead. The yeoman, who was armed only with a halbert, came to the ready and ordered the fugitives to halt. Blood, however, drew a pistol, and firing at close range knocked the man over.

Thus gaining free access to the drawbridge the party hastened over. On the far side, where stands the Middle Tower, was the Spur guard with its sentry posted. The man on duty at this moment was named Sill, a Cromwellian soldier now enlisted in the Royal Army. Cromwellian or no, he was not for being shot in cold blood, and seeing the warder fall, tactfully stepped aside and allowed the marauders to pass unhindered. Sir Gilbert Talbot thought he had been previously bribed by Blood, and this is not an unlikely explanation. Anyway, the chief obstacles had been overcome and the Crown and Orb were outside the main fortress. From the Middle Tower, Blood and his companions instead of going out of the Bulwark Gate a few yards off, doubled on their tracks, so to speak, and hastened along the wharf in an easterly direction towards the Iron Gate. This was a tactical error which proved fatal, for the wharf is some three hundred yards long and in full view throughout of the sentries standing on the battlements of the outer ballium wall.

By this time there seem to have been a considerable number of people on the wharf, some pursuing from behind, and some just entered through the Iron Gate on their ordinary business. These latter, seeing a commotion and hearing cries of treason and murder, with great zeal and promptitude, incited and directed by Blood, fell on the pursuers, and nearly murdered Captain Beckman, whom the worthy parson pointed out as the arch culprit.

Having disentangled himself from this awkward misconception, the gallant captain raced on along the wharf and came up with Blood just as he was getting to horse. Blood turned short and point blank fired his second pistol at Beckman's head. But a pistol in those days took some time to go off, which gave the captain time to duck his head and, charging low, to seize the reverend gentleman. A severe struggle then took place. The captain thinking more of the Crown itself than of the man who held it, instead of overpowering him tried to snatch the Crown from him. Blood resisted lustily but Beckman prevailed, and thus roughly handled he secured it. But naturally the stones being much loosened by the previous hammering, several here also fell out, though eventually all with a few comparatively insignificant exceptions were recovered.

Blood and Parrett were now overpowered and captured, whilst Hunt, who was Blood's son-in-law, though he got to horse, in galloping off hit his head against a pole sticking out from a laden wagon, and being dismounted was also captured. The three were immediately placed in the securest dungeons in the Tower, and word was sent to Sir Gilbert Talbot, the Keeper of the Jewel House, who at once informed the King. Those looking for a lurid and sanguinary end to this story will be disappointed. Considering the time and the penalties which were exacted on such comparatively venal offences as the stealing of sheep, one is naturally prepared to hear that Colonel Blood and his accomplices were at the shortest notice drawn on hurdles to Tyburn and there hanged, drawn, and quartered. But Fate plays curious tricks with the lives of men. The Merry Monarch, instead of being in the least annoyed with this audacious attempt which so nearly lost him his regal emblems, roared with laughter and ordered that the chief culprit should be sent for judgment to the highest court in the realm, the King himself.

What the King said to Blood, or what Blood said to the King, as variously chronicled, may be passed over, but the net result was that Blood instead of being executed was given a post amongst the bodyguard of His Majesty, and also granted a salary of £500 a year for life. As money was then five times

the value it was in 1914 and ten times the value it
is in 1920, we may estimate this as a very handsome
income.   Several reasons have been given for
Charles II's liberality, and each may be accepted
with equal caution. The wits and scandal-mongers
of the time declared that the explanation of the
King's leniency was due to one of two causes. The
first was that being as usual short of cash, His
Majesty conceived the novel expedient of stealing
his own Crown, and in a roundabout way put up
Blood to execute the project. The second was more
sporting than venal, and averred that the King
in one of his genial after-dinner moments had
declared that no one would, after the horrors of the
past, deprive him of his Crown, and had backed
his opinion by a bet.   This, so the story went,
having come to Blood's ears, he determined to
take up the bet literally and steal the actual emblems
of royalty.   These, though interesting explanations,
may in the absence of proof be relegated to uncon-
firmed gossip. However, the most charitable version
is little less astonishing. We are invited to believe
that the King believed Blood's fairy tale, which was
that he had laid out in the reeds close to the place
where the King was wont to bathe intending to
shoot him, when he had assumed the primitive garb
of his ancestor Adam, but that when the moment
came to pull the trigger, this hardened old soldier
was so overcome with the glory of the King's royal

body *in statu natura* that his finger absolutely refused to work.

Charles II, though jovial, was by no means an idiot; indeed he was one of the astutest monarchs who has sat on the throne of England. We may therefore perhaps brush aside all these interesting stories and arrive at the plain conclusion that the King, knowing from recent experience how precarious in those days was the life of a King, decided that his best policy was to take into his service a quondam and potential enemy, thereby turning a spear that threatened him into a defensive javelin. That shrewd lesson in statescraft has been followed, perhaps unwittingly, by the British Empire in its expansion. Times out of number in Asia, Africa, and America, the foes of one day have been on the next enrolled under the standards of the King of England, and alongside men of his own blood have fought the battles of the Empire.

Blood, contrary to the report that he was a mere burglar, the son of a blacksmith, and so forth, was in fact a man of good family residing at Sarney, Co. Meath, and was himself at the early age of twenty-two made a Justice of the Peace, itself a proof of his social standing. His grandfather was Edmund Blood of Kilnaboy Castle, Co. Clare, who was at one time M.P. for Ennis.

Perhaps the best estimate of Colonel Blood is that he was a hot-headed and fearless Irishman, who found it difficult to live quietly, and must ever work off his boundless energy on some new and often desperate enterprise. He was the Charles O'Malley of an earlier century, and demonstrated his Irish exuberance with rapier and pistol rather than in the hunting field.

Note.—The account of Colonel Blood's attempt on the Crown is taken from an ancient MS., written in 1680 at the dictation of Sir Gilbert Talbot, the Keeper of the Jewel House at the time, which is now in possession of Mrs. Lowndes, of Chesham, Bucks. A copy of the same document is also owned by General Sir Bindon Blood, G.C.B., together with other interesting records of Colonel Blood, which he has kindly placed at the writer's disposal.

CHAPTER XII

THE ORDERS OF CHIVALRY

TOGETHER with the King's Treasure in the Jewel House are kept the insignia of the Orders of Chivalry as well as decorations for bravery in battle.

The oldest of these is the Order of the Garter,

which was created by Edward III as far back as the year 1348. It is rather English that so ancient and highly esteemed an honour should owe its origin to quite a trivial incident. A lady, the Countess of Salisbury, who was dancing with the King at a Court Ball, dropped her garter. In this less emotional age nobody would be greatly amused if a lady dropped her garter; probably few would even notice it, unless perchance it happened to be set with diamonds. But in 1348 very small jokes apparently went a long way, and the dropping of this particular lady's garter caused vast amusement amongst the gallants. A garter is a garter, and there is evidently nothing either indecent or improper or even amusing about it; it is merely an article used by a few people now, and most people of both sexes in those days, to keep their stockings from slipping down.

However, there was the garter on the floor, and the fine gentlemen sniggering at it, whilst the poor lady who owned this harmless article was covered with confusion. In this tremendous crisis the King with a courtesy lacking amongst his courtiers stepped forward, picked up the garter, tied it round his own knee, and uttered the well-known rebuke, " Honi soit qui mal y pense." For English Kings spoke French in those days.

Edward III. was a gentleman, and it is not a little interesting to find that the oldest Order, not only in England but in the world, owes its origin to a little act of courtesy. In ancient days the Order was termed a Fraternity of Knights, and these were chosen by the King from amongst the most noble of those about the Royal person. They were not necessarily warriors of the sword, but must be Gentlemen of the Blood, such as the King thought fit to wear the same emblem as himself. A Gentleman of the Blood, it is explained, was one who could claim three descents in the *noblesse*, both on his father's and also his mother's side.

In bestowing the Garter the exhortation used was : " Sir, the loving Company of the Order of the Garter hath received you their Brother, Lover, and Fellow, and in token and knowledge of this, they give you and present you with this present Garter, the which God will that you receive and wear henceforth to his praise and pleasure and to the exaltation and honour of the said Most Noble Order and of yourself."

No person who had been convicted of error against the Christian faith, or of high treason, or of cowardice in face of the enemy could become a Knight of the Garter. And if being already a Knight he was guilty of either of these three " Reproaches," his spurs were cut off, his banner removed, and he was summarily expelled from the Order. The only other grave offence mentioned is for appearing without his Garter, the penalty for which was a fine of one mark ! Evidently, however, it was found that the Garter could not conveniently be worn with

N

long boots, so by special enactment a Knight so booted might wear a blue silk riband instead.

Later on the Order somewhat changed its character, for it came to be bestowed not only on persons of high lineage as such, but also on those who had reached places of eminence in the public service, like Thomas Cromwell, Earl of Essex, whose father was a shearer. As we come still further down in the ages we find it established, as at present, that though a number of vacancies in the Order are reserved for peers of the realm, yet it is also conferred as the very highest distinction attainable on soldiers, sailors, and statesmen who have done very conspicuous service to the State, whatever their lineage.

Exclusive of Royal personages, there are only twenty-five Knights of the Garter. The King is Sovereign of the Order, and some fourteen foreign Kings, English and foreign Princes, are amongst the Royal Knights. These include the Prince of Wales, the Duke of York, the Duke of Connaught, Prince Arthur of Connaught, the King of Spain, the King of Norway, the King of Italy, and the King of Denmark.

Until recently the German Emperor figured amongst the Knights, but his banner was taken down and his name removed from the Order in knightly disapproval of the unknightly manner in which the Germans were held to have waged war on land and sea. The name of the Emperor of Russia has also disappeared from the roll, through his tragic death. Amongst the great soldiers who won their spurs in the field were the Duke of Marlborough, the Duke of Wellington, Earl Roberts, and Earl Kitchener. The only two Ladies of the Order are Queen Mary and Queen Alexandra.

The Chapel of the Knights of the Garter is St. George's Chapel at Windsor Castle, and there may be seen the stalls of the Knights with their banners suspended over them.   When a Knight dies or is degraded, his banner is removed and that of his successor is hoisted in its place, whilst a small brass plate is left as a lasting record of each succeeding Knight in each of the stalls.

The Garter itself is of blue ribbon edged with gold, and has a buckle and pendent of gold richly chased.   Round the Garter in gold is the motto of the Order, " Honi soit qui mal y pense."   The Garter is worn below the left knee by a Knight, and round the left arm above the elbow by a Lady.

The Mantle or Robe is of blue velvet, of a shade which has come to be known as garter blue, on the left breast of which the Star is embroidered.   It is lined with white taffeta, and has a crimson velvet hood.   The surcoat is also of crimson velvet, lined with white taffeta.

The Hat is a very imposing affair made of black velvet and of a curious shape.   The plume is of white ostrich feathers with a tuft of black heron's feathers in the centre. It is fastened to the hat by a band of diamonds.

The Collar consists of a string of gold and enamelled red roses, from which hangs a presentment of St. George attacking the dragon. Across his breast the Knight wears the broad riband of the Order, from which is pendent a lesser presentiment of the same incident, which is known as the Badge.

The Star is eight-pointed and made of silver, though it is not unusual for a Knight, or his generous friends, to substitute a diamond star. Such a diamond Star was presented by his friends to Lord Roberts, and the Mary's of the Empire gave a similar token of their regard to Queen Mary.

A Knight of the Garter is the only Knight who wears his Star in evening dress at a private dinner party. All other Knights only wear their stars on such special occasions as are laid down, but always when asked to meet royalties. In this connection it may be interesting to mention that though a Knight may belong to many Orders, he only wears the Star of the senior one at these parties. If he were in uniform he would, of course, wear all he possessed, as may be gathered from the photographs of celebrated admirals and field-marshals which are to be seen in the illustrated papers.

The Order of the Thistle claims a very ancient origin, for though it was only organised as a knightly fraternity by James II in 1687, the Royal Warrant issued by that monarch mentions that " His Majesty's royal predecessor, Achaius King of Scots, did institute the most ancient and the most noble Order of the Thistle, under the protection of St. Andrew, Patron of Scotland : in commemoration of a signal Victory obtained by the said Achaius over Athelstan, King of the Saxons, after a bloody battle, in the time of which there appeared in the heavens a White Cross in the form of that upon which the Apostle Saint Andrew suffered martyrdom." When James II abdicated, the Order fell into desuetude, but was again revived by Queen Anne in 1703.

The Mantle is of green velvet, with the Badge of the Order embroidered on the left side. The Riband of the Order is green. The Star of this Order consists of a St. Andrew's Cross laid on a silver star. In the centre of this combination is a Thistle of green and gold upon a field of gold, surrounded by a circle of green, bearing the motto of the Order, " Nemo me impure lacessit." The Collar is formed of thistles intermingled with sprigs of rue, and from it pendent is the Badge or Jewel, representing St. Andrew wearing a green gown and purple surcoat, and bearing before him a white enamelled cross.

The Order consists of the Sovereign and sixteen Knights, one of the most recent of whom, it may be remembered, is Field-Marshal Earl Haig.

The Thistle was a most expensive Order in ancient days, the fees on admission amounting to £347, a very considerable sum at that time. Edward VII reduced this to £50, which is the sum now paid by a Knight to the Treasury on admission to the Order.

The Order of St. Patrick is of more recent origin, and owes its inception to George III in 1783. It is an Irish Order modelled on the Fraternity of the Knights of the Garter, and was intended to emphasise the unity of the United Kingdom. To further which idea the new Order was given the motto, "Quis separabit?" A pertinent inquiry to which Sinn Feiners and other extraordinary persons have since made constant endeavours to return a disloyal reply.

The Mantle is of Irish tabbinet of a very beautiful shade of light blue, and is lined with white silk. On the right shoulder is a blue hood of the same material lined also with white silk. On the left side is embroidered the Star of the Order. The Collar is of gold composed of roses and harps alternately, and at the bottom is a harp surmounted by an Imperial Crown. The Badge is of gold of an oval form, in the centre of which is a trefoil with three crowns, standing on the cross of St. Patrick and surrounded with a wreath of shamrock. Round the wreath is the motto of the Order.

The Star consists of the Cross of St. Patrick gules,

on a field argent, surmounted by a trefoil vert, charged with three Imperial Crowns with a circle of azure containing the motto, " Quis separabit ? " and the date " MDCCLXXXIII " in letters of gold. The whole is encircled by four greater and four lesser rays of silver. This Star also can at the expense of the Knight or his friends be fashioned in diamonds. The Riband is light blue and is worn across the breast from left to right, the Badge being worn at the tie over the left thigh.

The Order of Merit has a somewhat curious origin. There were, and are, certain Englishmen of the very highest eminence who are averse to being other than plain " Mr." to the end of their days. Peerages, baronetcies, and knighthoods have no attraction for them. Such men were Mr. Joseph Chamberlain and Mr. Gladstone, and such to-day is Mr. Arthur Balfour. The feeling is a noble one and quite in accordance with the best traditions of the English character. King Edward VII, in the hope of finding an acceptable road, therefore instituted the Order of Merit, which carries no title with it and no precedence. To make the Order exceedingly select and highly prized the number of members may not exceed twenty-four, and it is open only to those who have performed exceptional meritorious services in the navy, army, art, literature, and science. The King may also bestow the honour as extra members on foreigners of distinction.

The Badge of the Order consists of a Cross of red and blue enamel of eight points, with the addition of cross swords in the case of a naval or military officer. On it is a laurel wreath upon a centre of blue enamel, and the motto of the Order "For Merit," in letters of gold. On the reverse, within laurel leaves on blue enamel, is the cipher of King Edward in gold. Above is the Imperial Crown enamelled in proper colours. The riband of the Order is parti-coloured, garter blue and crimson.

One of the latest recipients of the Order is Mr. Lloyd George, and other distinguished members are Field-Marshal Viscount French, Viscount Morley, Sir William Crookes, Thomas Hardy, Sir Archibald Geikie, Mr. Arthur Balfour, and Field-Marshal Earl Haig.

The Order confers no precedence, but the initials O.M. are authorised to be placed after the G.C.B. and before all other initials. What happens when the wife of an O.M. meets at a dinner party the wife of a G.C.S.I. opens up a vista of precedental problems which the Lord Chamberlain's office could alone solve.

Next to the Garter the Order of the Bath is the most ancient and most honourable. Indeed, the Bath is entitled "The Most Honourable Order," and though it has precedence below the Garter, Thistle, and St. Patrick, it is in some respects superior to these, for it can only be earned in reward for services rendered. It is also older than any other Order in the world except the Garter, being some fifty years older than the Order of the Golden Fleece. It was said by a foreigner, that any English title or decoration could be bought except the Order of the Bath. That is a somewhat sweeping assertion, though we ourselves allow that one of the blots on English public life is that peerages, baronetcies, and knighthoods can be, and are, bought from the political party in power. Happily it is still, as from the beginning, impossible to buy the Order of the Bath. Probably this fact, as well as its ancient and knightly origin, gives the Order its high standing, and we may venture to hope that it will never be otherwise.

It is not perhaps generally known that the Order of the Bath literally came from the common or domestic hip-bath. Long before this Order was instituted it was customary for warriors, who led in those times very strenuous days and nights, fighting, eating and drinking, and making love, to take a warm bath the night before they were knighted. This ablution had partly a temporal and partly a spiritual significance. It was not, however, till 1399 that Henry IV determined to make a permanent institution of an Order for Knights of the Sword, and named it the Order of the Bath. '

Space does not allow of giving the full ritual,

which may be read elsewhere,[1] but the actual taking of a warm bath was one of the leading features. This bath was taken in the large hall adjoining St. John's Chapel in the White Tower, Tower of London. Whilst the Knight was in his bath the King came in accompanied by prelates and noblemen, and dipping his finger in the water made a cross on the Knight's back.

A curious complication arose in this connection when a Queen, in the person of Mary I, came to the throne, for naturally she could not go about making crosses on the backs of naked young Knights. But both in Queen Mary's reign and in that of Queen Elizabeth the difficulty was tided over by delegating a nobleman of high rank to act for the Queen.

On the King's departure the Knight was put into a bed to dry and warm, bath towels apparently being little known in those days. Having thus become dry and warm the Knight put on a monk's frock and then proceeded into St. John's Chapel, where he watched his arms all night. On the morrow he rode in procession with other Knights of the Bath before the King to Westminster. This custom has long been discontinued; the Knight takes his bath at home as usual, and then proceeds to Buckingham Palace and is there Knighted by the King.

Originally there was one grade in the Order, that of Knight, but now there are three grades : Grand

[1] See *The Tower from Within*, Chapter VIII.

Cross, Knight Commander, and Companion. Up to 1847 only soldiers and sailors distinguished in war could be appointed, thus keeping up the knightly heritage; moreover they must have been mentioned in despatches, and must be field officers or of corresponding rank in the navy. In 1847 the Order was made more elastic so as to include civilians who had done eminent service to the State, and also it was opened to distinguished foreigners. The insignia, however, for a civilian member is different from that of a military member, though the ribands are the same. Here has resulted a very curious anomaly. After the Waterloo campaign the Order of the Bath was swept and garnished, so to speak, and amongst other innovations the insignia was remade in the shape of an eight-pointed cross, much on the lines of the Legion of Honour, inaugurated by Napoleon I. When the civil division was introduced in 1847 the insignia assigned was an oval gold medallion, having a trefoil in open work in the centre. This insignia, thus revived, must have been the old and original emblem worn by Knights of the Bath from very ancient days. An old engraving for instance of the Black Prince shows this very form of medallion round his neck.

A Grand Cross of the Bath wears a robe of red silk with the badge of the Order embroidered on the left side, and the collar of the Order. He also alone wears the broad riband across his chest with the badge at the tie, and a special Star. A Knight Commander wears a smaller star on the left side of his coat, and the insignia of the Order round his neck. A Companion wears only the insignia, of a smaller size, round his neck. Members of the three grades carry after their names the initials G.C.B., K.C.B., and C.B.

Next in precedence to the Bath comes the Star of India, though it dates only from 1861, an interval of nearly 500 years. The precedence thus given was probably a matter of policy after the Indian Mutiny, the Order having, it is expressly stated, been inaugurated for the purpose of rendering high honour to conspicuous loyalty and merit amongst the princes, chiefs, and people of the Indian Empire. The Order is, however, open not only to Indians, but to Englishmen who have performed distinguished service in, or connected with, India.

As in the case of the Bath, this Order is divided into three grades: Grand Commander, Knight Commander, and Companion. It will be noticed that the word " Commander " is used instead of " Cross " in the highest grade. This was out of deference to the Mahomedan subjects of the sovereign, for to a Mahomedan the cross is a Christian symbol, and as such, like ham and bacon, a thing to be avoided.

The Robe of the Grand Commander is of light blue silk with the Badge of the Order embroidered on the left side. The riband, stars, and insignia are

worn by the three grades as described for the
Order of the Bath.

The insignia is a very beautiful and valuable
jewel. It consists of an onyx cameo, having in the
centre the effigy of Queen Victoria. This is set in an
oval gold band which contains the motto, " Heaven's
Light our Guide," in diamonds. The three grades
are distinguished by the initials G.C.S.I., K.C.S.I.,
and C.S.I. On the death of a member of the Order,
his insignia have to be returned, unless his heirs
consent to purchase them.

After the Napoleonic wars, for some reason which
seems now somewhat obscure, the King, or the
Government, or both, appear to have been at their
wits' end to discover an appropriate medium by
which marks of the royal favour might be suitably
conferred upon the natives of Malta and the Ionian
Islands. Out of the travail thus begotten emerged
the Most Distinguished Order of St. Michael and
St. George. Indeed, so pronouncedly foreign was it
intended to be that instead of Companions the
members were termed Cavalieri of the Order. After
struggling along for fifty years in Malta and the
Ionian Islands, an Order of little repute or standing,
Queen Victoria decided to give it a wider scope and
to throw it open to the whole Empire. After this
happy inspiration the Order grew and prospered,
first as a purely civil and colonial decoration, but
latterly chiefly as a military Order, second only in

value and public estimation to the Order of the Bath.

The mantle or robe of a Grand Cross is of Saxon blue satin, lined with scarlet, having on the left side embroidered the Star of the Order. The Collar is suitably formed of a chain of Lions of England and Maltese Crosses, alternately. The Star has seven rays of silver, between each of which is a small ray of gold ; over all the Cross of St. George, gules. In the centre of the said star is a circle azure whereon is inscribed in letters of gold the motto of the Order, " Auspicium Melioris," and the figure of St. Michael with flaming sword trampling on Satan. " Auspicium Melioris " may freely be translated, " There is a good time coming," or perhaps more sedately, " The promise of a better age."

On one side of the Badge may be seen St. George slaying the Dragon, and on the other St. Michael trampling on Satan. The members of the three grades wear their insignia as laid down for the Bath, and are styled G.C.M.G., K.C.M.G., and C.M.G.

The Order of the Indian Empire was instituted by Queen Victoria on January 1st, 1878, to commemorate the proclamation of Her Majesty as Empress of India, a title then first added to the British Crown. It was to be bestowed as a reward to those who from time to time were held to have rendered important services to the Indian Empire. At first it was bestowed mostly on civilians, but latterly its scope has been broadened, and it is now given for military services as well.

It may be noticed that whereas the Order of the Bath, which was a purely military Order, was after nearly five hundred years opened to civilians, Orders like the Star of India, St. Michael and St. George, and the Indian Empire, started on exactly opposite lines; they were intended for civilians only. But happily now all these Orders are open alike to soldiers, sailors, and civilians who have done in their own lines good service to their King and Empire, and that is really all that matters.

The robe or mantle of a Grand Cross is of purple satin lined with white silk, having on the left side embroidered the Star of the Order. The Collar is Oriental in treatment forming a chain of elephants, lotus flowers, peacocks in their pride, and Indian roses, all in gold. The elephants nearly caused an upheaval in a later reign, and the story shows how easily insurrections are caused amongst so seemingly a docile people as the Indians. When the design for the coinage of George V was being decided upon it seemed not inappropriate that the King should be shown crowned, and wearing the mantle of the Order of the Indian Empire with the Collar round his neck. Rupees to the number of many hundred thousands were consequently struck with this presentiment of the King on them. Hardly were these in circulation when some lynx-eyed political agitator discovered that the King was wearing the effigy of a pig round his neck, and as a pig, even in silver, is anathema to a Mahomedan it was put about by pernicious persons that a calculated insult had thus been thrust in the most blatant and enduring form on the whole Mahomedan population. It was quite useless for the Government to assert and vow that the animal portrayed was not a pig but an elephant, and that if they looked at the original chain there could be no possible doubt about it. The Mahomedan agitators were impervious to persuasion, nothing in the wide world would persuade them that it was not a pig, probably secretly inserted by some subtle Bengali employed at the mint. Their co-religionists refused to accept or use this rupee in trade, and so the Government had to recall the whole issue from circulation and had it melted down and recoined with the obnoxious chain eliminated.

The Star is of silver, ten pointed, and has in the centre a medallion of Queen Victoria, around which is a dark blue garter surmounted by an imperial crown. In gold on the garter is the motto of the Order, "Imperatricis Auspicus," which being broadly interpreted is "Honored by the Empress."

The Badge is heraldically described as a Rose enamelled gules barbed vert, having in the centre the effigy of Queen Victoria. The subaltern who knows nothing of heraldry, and describes things bluntly as they strike him, wavers between likening it to a jam tart or a squashed tomato, when suddenly faced with this emblem on the broad chest of his general. Many, however, think this a very effective decoration emblematic of the Victorian era.

There are, as in the case of the Bath, three grades of this Order, the hall marks of which are G.C.I.E., K.C.I.E., and C.I.E., and each of these in their degree wear stars and insignia in diminishing degree as with other Orders.

The Royal Victorian Order was created by Queen Victoria in 1896 for bestowal by the sovereign upon those whose personal services it might be desired to recognise. There are five classes in this Order ranging from Knights Grand Cross to Members of the Fifth Class, so that all social grades can receive a suitable decoration. The Prince of Wales may be at one end and a Highland gillie at the other. King Edward added a Royal Victorian Chain to the Order which is only bestowed on very special occasions. There is no mantle or robe to this Order. The Badge is in the form of a cross of white enamel, in the centre of which is a medallion having Queen Victoria's cipher in the middle, and the word Victoria on a blue enamel garter round the cipher. Above is an imperial crown in enamel proper. The Stars of the Grand Cross and Knight Commander of the Order are of silver and of different patterns and sizes.

o

The Order of the British Empire was instituted by George V during the Great War, for the purpose of rewarding those engaged in war work away from the fighting line. Men and women are equally eligible for all the five classes of this Order. It is understood that after the services rendered in the late war have received recognition the Order may fall into abeyance and no further addition made to its members. The Star is of silver with a medallion in the centre in red enamel on which is the figure in gold of Britannia seated. Around is the motto of the Order, " For God and the Empire." The Badge is in the form of a cross of grey enamel and in the centre is the same medallion as on the Star. The ribbon of civil members is purple, and that for military members the same, but with a red line down the centre.

The only Order reserved entirely for Ladies is the Crown of India. It was inaugurated at the same time as the Order of the Indian Empire, and to commemorate the same event, the assumption of the title of Empress of India by Queen Victoria. The Ladies eligible for this Order are princesses of the Royal House, the wives or female relatives of Indian Princes, and other Indian ladies of high degree. Amongst Englishwomen eligibility is restricted to the wives, or in the case of a bachelor the sister, of the Viceroy of India, the Governors of Bengal, Madras and Bombay, and the Secretary of State for India. The

Order is therefore very select indeed, and one may make a long night's march through the ballrooms and dining-rooms of the world without seeing one. The decoration itself is a beautiful one and worthy to be worn by any lady, however great. The Badge consists of an oval buckle set round with pearls closely touching. In the centre is the cipher of Queen Victoria, the " V " being set with diamonds, the " R " with pearls, and the " I " with turquoises. Above the oval buckle is an Imperial Crown enamelled proper. The Badge hangs pendant from a light blue silk bow. The Order is worn on the left breast.

A quiet-looking and quietly dressed lady was one day looking at the Crown Jewels, and especially the Orders. When she came to the Crown of India the official showing her round made the time-honoured joke that to obtain this beautiful jewel she had only to marry a Viceroy. " I have already done so," remarked the quiet lady, and passed on. She was the wife of a late Viceroy.

The most highly prized decoration in the Army or Navy is the Victoria Cross. This was instituted by Queen Victoria after the Crimean War for the purpose of rewarding individual cases of conspicuous gallantry in presence of the enemy. Hitherto the only war decoration that could be won by an individual solider or sailor was the Order of the Bath, and by the rules of that order no officer below the

rank of major, or of equivalent rank in the Navy,
could be recommended for it. Queen Victoria's
intention was that the Victoria Cross should be open
to all from admiral or general to bugler boy or sailor
boy. " Neither rank, nor long service, nor wounds,
nor any other circumstance or condition whatsoever
save the merit of conspicuous bravery (in the
presence of the enemy) shall be held to establish a
sufficient claim to the honour." [1]

The Victoria Cross, like all decorations, has had
its ups and downs, but there is not the least doubt
that during the Great War it has upheld its highest
traditions. During its middle history the decoration
was perhaps more popular with the public than
with the military, for soldiers in action saw how
often it was a pure matter of luck that one should get
the Cross and another not. The interpretation of
the Warrant also varied, for whereas some generals
in the field were very chary about recommending
anyone, others were most liberal. In the South
African War a sumptuary law was passed that no
one above the rank of captain should be recommended, and thus several well-known officers of
higher rank were ruled out and given the Bath
instead. This probably came from reading the first
part of the Warrant which emphasises the eligibility
of the junior ranks for the Bath, without reading
the context above quoted.

[1] Victoria Cross Warrant, 1856.

Again at one period nobody could hope to get the Victoria Cross unless he had assisted a wounded man under fire ; it came for a time at any rate to take the position of a life-saving medal on land, as is the Humane Society's medal for saving life from the water. Indeed so obsessed did some become with this strange doctrine that Lord Roberts himself had the greatest difficulty in obtaining the Victoria Cross for two very gallant officers at Kabul in 1879, because their gallantry had no connection with carrying wounded men out of action.

With these vagaries before them it is not to be wondered at that the Victoria Cross for some years lost its value amongst officers, indeed it was openly discussed whether it would not be wiser to reserve the Cross for the N.C.O.'s and men in the ranks only, and to make all officers ineligible. This on the grounds that all, or anyway the majority of British officers, are brave and that it was a pity to draw invidious distinctions. The Great War has, however, as we have seen, thoroughly rehabilitated the Victoria Cross, for though there certainly are hundreds who with better luck would have received it, yet those who have obtained it have set a very high standard of gallantry in face of the enemy.

The Cross itself is familiar to all. It is a plain bronze Maltese Cross, with a Lion standing on a Crown in the centre, and the words " For Valour " inscribed beneath. The actual cost of the Cross is threepence. The ribbon is red for all branches of His Majesty's Service whether on sea, or land, or the air. When the ribbon is worn in undress a miniature V.C. is placed on it, and should there be clasps to the V.C. for each one a miniature is added. Until recently the Navy had a blue ribbon, but when the Air Force came into being the King thought it better to have one and the same ribbon for all.

In precedence the Victoria Cross ranks before all decorations and medals and is worn on the right of all. Thus in addressing a letter to one who has the Victoria Cross the letters V.C. precede all others, even if the addressee is a Knight of the Garter or a Grand Cross of the Bath. All those not of commissioned rank who are decorated with the Victoria Cross are given a special pension of £10 a year, and for each bar £5 extra per annum.[1]

The Distinguished Service Order was inaugurated in 1886 by Queen Victoria, and at the time the general impression in the services was that it was intended to be in the nature of a second grade of the Victoria Cross. This was a mistake, for the Order was really instituted as a second grade to the Bath. Experience in our numberless small wars had shown that many junior officers performed distinguished service, but being ineligible for the Bath got nothing. The new Order was to be granted to officers irrespective of rank for " meritorious and distinguished service in war."

[1] These have been lately considerably increased.

From the very beginning, in the Burmah War of 1886–87, a very wide interpretation of these words was used, and though the D.S.O. was given for deeds of gallantry and devotion in action it was also given to those who had done meritorious service far far away from the sound of guns. With this precedent the Order ran downhill at a great pace till it got to be known as the " Doing Something-or-Other Order." All sorts and conditions of people got it, sometimes with but the faintest glimmer of merit or distinction. The Great War has, however, to a great extent improved the status of the Order, and if only the present high standard is maintained it will undoubtedly rise to the position it was originally intended to occupy.

The decoration is in the form of an eight-pointed gold cross the wings of which are covered with white enamel. In the centre is the Imperial Crown in gold on a red enamel background round which is a wreath of green enamel laurels. The ribbon is crimson with narrow borders of blue. If an officer gets a clasp to his D.S.O. a small silver rose is placed on the ribbon when worn in undress uniform and an additional rose is added for each subsequent clasp. The decoration is open to officers of all ranks both in the Army and the Navy.

A decoration which came into being during the Great War is that of Companions of Honour. This decoration, like the Order of Merit, is bestowed on those who for various reasons are averse to receiving any reward from the Sovereign which carries a title.

The Military Cross and its naval equivalent, the Distinguished Service Cross, were products of the Great War. In former wars we had engaged a few tens of thousands of fighting men, but in the Great War we had seven million soldiers and sailors engaged all over the world.[1] In the great battles that took place during four and a half years of this gigantic conflict thousands of officers distinguished themselves, yet all could not be given the Victoria Cross or the Distinguished Service Order. A third decoration for gallantry thus became imperative. The Military Cross for the Army and the Distinguished Service Cross for the Navy were the outcome of this demand, and all officers and warrant officers are elegible for them; they are both of silver, but differ somewhat in design. The ribbons are somewhat similar, but in the case of the Military Cross the centre stripe is purple and the two outside ones white; whilst with the Distinguished Service Cross, the white stripe is in the middle and the two outer ones are purple. When an officer or warrant officer earns one or more clasps, a small silver rose is placed on the ribbon for each clasp.

During the Great War the gallantry and achievements of the Air Force called imperatively for

[1] Eighteen million medals are in course of being struck.

special recognition. This was met by instituting two decorations open only to the Air Force. These are the Distinguished Flying Cross, for bestowal upon officers in the Royal Air Force for acts of gallantry when flying in active operations against the enemy; and the Air Force Cross, for bestowal on officers of the Royal Air Force for acts of courage or devotion to duty when flying, although not in active operations, against the enemy.

We now come to those decorations which are reserved for warrant and non-commissioned officers and the rank and file, and for which no officer as such is eligible. Naturally any soldier or sailor who had won one of these decorations when in the ranks or the lower deck would carry it on with him and wear it on all occasions if he subsequently received a commission. The first of these is for the Army, the Distinguished Conduct Medal, familiar to all as the D.C.M.; and for the Navy the Conspicuous Gallantry Medal, generally known as the C.G.M. The second pair under the category are the Military Medal for the soldiers, and the Distinguished Service Medal for the sailors. These are known as the M.M. and D.S.M.

All these four medals are round silver insignia of the familiar size and shape of a war medal. On one side they have the King's head and shoulders, in a Field-Marshal's uniform, for the Army, and in that of an Admiral of the Fleet for the Navy. On the other side is the designation of the medal. Should a soldier or a sailor be granted one of these medals a second time the fact would be marked by the addition of a silver clasp.

The ribbons of these decorations are: For the D.C.M. red and blue. The D.S.M. (Naval) has blue and white. The ribbon for the Military Medal is red white and blue, and that of the C.G.M. (Naval) blue and white.

It will be noticed that since 1856 the number of British Orders and decorations has very greatly increased. At that date there were only the Garter, the Thistle, St. Patrick, the Bath, and the Michael and George, and only the last two of these was open to ordinary persons. Now there are upwards of twenty Orders and decorations open to those who do good and valiant service for the Empire in peace and war. As is only natural, opinions are divided on the subject. Several millions of His Majesty's subjects who have not received one of these insignia of honour decry the whole system, and say it is debasing to wear decorations for doing one's duty. Several millions more hope, given the opportunity, to earn one of them; whilst the few thousands who have received them feel, in a greater or less degree, a certain warm sense of gratification in that their King and country have discovered what fine fellows they are.

The increase in the number of Orders and decorations is mainly due to the great extension of the Empire, the wars both great and small that have been waged during the past seventy years, and the impossibility of rewarding the greatly increased numbers of those whom the King delighteth to honour with practically only one Order open for a restricted distribution, the Order of the Bath. After so great a war as the Great War, wherein many millions of men of British blood were engaged, naturally all the now existing Orders are full to over-flowing with members and supernumerary members, but as the river runs low after the heavy rains are over, so will the flow of honours decrease to the small stream which in peace time can alone keep up their value.

APPENDIX A

KEEPERS OF THE JEWEL HOUSE[1]

Abbot and Monks of Westminster, 1042–66, in the reign of Edward the Confessor.

First official Keeper of the Regalia, 1216, in the reign of Henry III.

Bishop of Carlisle, 1230, in the reign of Henry III.

John de Flete, 1337, in the reign of Edward III.

Robert de Mildenhall, 1347, in the reign of Edward III.

Thomas Chitterne, 1418, in the reign of Henry VI.

" The two Cary's," both Privy Councillors.

Thomas Cromwell, Earl of Essex, 1531–34, in the reign of Henry VIII.

John Williams, Lord Williams, 1539–44, in the reign of Henry VIII.

Richard Wilbraham of Woodhey, Cheshire, 1547 (?) to 1553, in the reign of Edward VI.

Marquis of Winchester, 1553, in the reign of Edward VI. Handed over the Crown Jewels to Lady Jane Grey.

[1] Named at various periods, Master and Treasurer of the Jewel House, Keeper of the Regalia, Keeper of the Crown Jewels, and as now Keeper of the Jewel House.

John Astley, 1558–95, in the reign of Queen Elizabeth.

Sir Henry Mildmay, 1622 (?)–1660, in the reigns of James I, Charles I, and interregnum.

Sir Gilbert Talbot, 1661–91, in the reign of Charles II, James II, and William and Mary.

Sir Francis Lawley, 1691–97, in the reign of William and Mary.

Heneage Mountague, 1697–98, in the reign of William and Mary.

Charles Godfrey, 1698–1716, in the reigns of William and Mary, Queen Anne, and George I.

Hon. James Brudenell, 1716–30, in the reigns of George I and George II.

Charles Townshend, Lord Lynn, 1730–39, in the reign of George II.

William Neville, Lord Abergavenny, 1739–45, in the reign of George II.

John Campbell, Lord Glenorchie, 1745–56, in the reign of George II.

Sir Richard Lyttleton, 1756–63, in the reigns of George II and George III.

Henry Vane, Earl of Darlington, 1763–82, in the reign of George III.

In 1782 the Office was suppressed and its duties transferred to the Lord Chamberlain (Stat. 22, Geo. III, c. 82). The Office was again revived early in the nineteenth century. At the Coronation of George IV, Thomas Baucutt Mash acted as " Officer of the Jewel House."

Lieut.-Colonel Charles Wyndham (late Scots Greys), 1852–72, in the reign of Queen Victoria.

Colonel John Cox Gawler (late 73rd Foot), 1872–82, in the reign of Queen Victoria.

Lieut.-General George Dean-Pitt, C.B., 1882–83, in the reign of Queen Victoria.

Captain Arthur John Loftus (late 10th Hussars) 1883–91, in the reign of Queen Victoria.

Lieut.-General Sir Michael Biddulph, G.C.B., 1891–96, in the reign of Queen Victoria.

Lieut.-General Sir Frederick Middleton, K.C.M.G., C.B., 1896–98, in the reign of Queen Victoria.

General Sir Hugh Gough, V.C., G.C.B., 1898–1909, in the reigns of Queen Victoria and Edward VII.

General Sir Robert Low, G.C.B., 1909–11, in the reign of Edward VII.

General Sir Arthur Wynne, G.C.B., 1911–17, in the reign of George V.

Major-General Sir George Younghusband, K.C.M.G., K.C.I.E., C.B., 1917 (present holder), in the reign of George V.

APPENDIX B

A letter written by Queen Anne Boleyn, when a prisoner in the Tower in the early part of May, 1536, to Henry VIII asking for mercy. This letter was apparently intercepted by Thomas Cromwell, Earl of Essex, and never reached the King. After Essex in his turn had been executed, some years later, Queen Anne Boleyn's letter was found in his portfolio amongst other papers.

From Queen Anne Boleyn to Henry VIII :

" SIR,—Your Grace's displeasure and my imprisonment are things so strange unto me as what to write or what to excuse I am altogether ignorant.

" Whereas you send unto me (willing me to confess a truth, and so to obtain your favour) by such an one whom you know to be mine antient professed enemy. I no sooner conceived this message by him than I rightly conceived your meaning : and if, as you say, confessing a truth indeed may procure my safety, I shall with all willingness and duty perform your command.

" But let not your Grace ever imagine that your poor wife will ever be brought to acknowledge a fault where not so much as a thought thereof proceeded. And to speak a truth, never prince had a wife more loyal in all duty and in all true affection, than you have ever found in Anne Boleyn ; with which name and place I could willingly have contented myself, if God and your Grace's pleasure had been so pleased. Neither did I at any time so far forget myself in my exaltation or received queenship, but that I always looked for such an alteration as now I find : for the ground of my preferment being on no surer foundation than your Grace's fancy, the least alteration, I knew, was fit and sufficient to draw that fancy to some other subject. You have chosen me from low estate to be your queen and companion, far beyond my desert or desire. If then you found me worthy of such honour, good your Grace, let not any light fancy or bad counsel of mine enemies, withdraw your princely favour from me ; neither let that stain, that unworthy stain, of a disloyal heart towards your good Grace, ever cast so foul a blot on your most dutiful wife and the infant princess your daughter.

" Try me good King, but let me have a lawful trial ; and let not my sworn enemies sit as my accusers and my judges ; yea, let me receive an open trial, for my truth shall fear no open shame. Then shall you see either my innocency cleared, your suspicions and conscience satisfied, the ignominy and slander of the world stopped, or my guilt lawfully declared ; so that whatsoever God or you

P

may determine of me, as your Grace may be freed from an open censure ; and mine offence being so openly proved, you Grace is at liberty, both before God and man, not only to execute your worthy punishment on me, as an unlawful wife, but to follow your affection already settled on that party for whose sake I am now as I am, whose name I could some good while since have pointed unto ; your Grace not being ignorant of my suspicion therein.

" But if you have already determined of me ; and that not only my death, but an infamous slander, must bring you the joying of your desired happiness ; then I desire of God that He will pardon your great sin therein, and likewise mine enemies, the instruments thereof ; and that He will not call you to a straight account for your unprincely and cruel usage of me, at His general judgment seat, where both you and myself must shortly appear ; and in whose judgment I doubt not, whatever the world may think of me, mine innocence shall be openly known and sufficiently cleared.

" My last and only request shall be, that myself may only bear the burden of your Grace's displeasure, and that it may not touch the innocent souls of those poor gentlemen, who, as I understand, are likewise in straight imprisonment for my sake. If ever I have found favour in your sight, if ever the name of Anne Boleyn hath been pleasing in your ears, then let me obtain this request ; and I will so leave to trouble your Grace any further ; with mine earnest prayers to the Trinity to have your Grace in His good keeping, and to direct you in all your actions. From my doleful prison in the Tower, this 6th of May. Your most loyal and ever faithful wife.

" ANNE BOLEYN."

APPENDIX C

Complete list of the Regalia in the Jewel House in A.D. 1920.

I. *Crowns and Diadem*—
1. King Edward the Confessor's Crown.
2. The Imperial State Crown.
3. The Imperial Indian Crown.
4. Crown of Queen Mary of Modena.
5. Crown of Queen Mary, Consort of King . George V.
6. Diadem of Queen Mary of Modena.
7. Crown of the Prince of Wales (as eldest son of the King).

II. *Sceptres and Rods*—
1. The King's Royal Sceptre.
2. The King's Sceptre with the Dove, or Rod of Equity.
3. The Queen's Sceptre with the Cross.
4. The Queen's Sceptre with the Ivory Dove.
5. James I's Sceptre with the Dove.
6. St. Edward's Staff.

III. *Orbs—*
    1. The King's Orb.
    2. The Queen's Orb.

IV. *Rings—*
    1. The King's Coronation Ring.
    2. The Queen's Coronation Ring.
    3. Queen Victoria's Coronation Ring.

V. *Swords—*
    1. The King's Jewelled State Sword.
    2. The Sword of State.
    3. The Sword Spiritual.
    4. The Sword Temporal.
    5. Curtana, or the Sword of Mercy.

VI. *Spurs and Bracelets—*
    1. St. George's Gold Spurs.
    2. Gold Bracelets.

VII. *Maces—*
    1. Charles II.
    2.   Do.
    3. James II.
    4.   Do.
    5. William and Mary.
    6.   Do.
    7.   Do.
    8. George I,

VIII. *Ecclesiastical Plate—*
    1. The Ampulla, or Golden Eagle.
    2. The Anointing Spoon.
    3. The Royal Baptismal Font of Charles II.
    4. Alms Dish of William and Mary.
    5. Chalice   Do.

IX. *State Trumpets and Banners—*
    1. Fifteen Silver State Trumpets.
    2. Twenty Bannerets.

X. *Royal Gold Plate—*
    1. Queen Elizabeth's Salt Cellar.
    2. King Charles II's Salt Cellar (State Cellar).
    3.   Do.
    4.   Do.
    5.   Do.
    6.   Do.
    7.   Do.
    8.   Do.
    9.   Do.
    10.   Do.
    11.   Do.
    12.   Do.
    13.   Do.
    14. King Charles II's Wine Fountain.
    15. Twelve Salt Spoons.
    16. Two Tankards (George IV).

XI. *Other Plate and Valuables—*
  1. The Maundy Dish of Charles II.
  2. King James II's Monde.
  3. Model of Koh-i-Nur Diamond with original setting.
  4. Model of Cullinan Diamond as found.
  5. Steel hammer and chisel, used in cutting the Cullinan Diamond.

APPENDIX D

" OF THE JEWELL HOUSE "

Copy of MSS. written or dictated by Sir Gilbert Talbot, Kt., appointed Keeper of the Jewel House, A.D. 1660–61, by Charles II. The original is in the possession of Mrs. Ethel M. Lowndes, The Bury, Chesham, Bucks.

Of the Jewell
House
With the ancient
rights
belonging
to the Maister &
Treasurer
thereof.

The Maister of ye Jewell H. holdeth his place by Patent, for life under the Broad Seale of England to enjoy all the perquisites and privileges wch any of his predecessors at any time enjoyed
which are as follows :

The Maister of ye Jewell H: holdeth his place by Patent for life under the Broad Seale of England. to enioy all the perquisites, and priviledges, wch. any of his predecessors at any time enioyed.

which are, as follow.

1. — A Fee of 50li. per an: out of the Exchecquer.

2. — A Table of 14 double dishes, p diem.

3. — 300. per an: out of ye New-yeares guift money.

4. — The carrying of Presents to Embassadours.

5. — The small presents at New yeares Tyde.

6. — Anciently Treasurers of ye Chambr. wch.

ch

w. office was a branch of y̆ Jewell ꝏ.

7. - Frequently Privy Counsaillers: as
Cromwell; & y̆ two Caryes.

8. - Right to buy, keep, & present all
his Ma^tys Jewells. (when given.)

9. - Choice of his under-Officers.

10. - Choice of the Kings and Queenes
Goldsmiths, & Jewellers.

11. - 20^li in gold. upon signing of the
Gold-smith's Bill.

12. Lodgings, in all y̆ K^gs Houses.

13. A Close-waggon (when y̆ Court
removeth) for his owne goodes; and
two carts for his officers.

14. Precedence, in Court & kingdome.

15. Priviledg of the drawing roome.

16. Robes at the Coronation.

17. In Procession, place before all
the Judges.

1. A Fee of 50£ per. an. out of the Exchequer.

2. A Table of 14 double dishes per diem.

3. 300£ per. an. out of ye New years guift money.

4. The carrying of Presents to Embassadours.

5. The small presents at New yeare's Tide.

6. Anciently Treasurers of ye Chamber wch office was a branch of ye Jewell H.

7. Frequently Privy Counsaillers as Cromwell & ye two Caryes.

8. Right to buy, keep & present all his Ma^{ts} Jewells (when given).

9. Choice of his under Officers.

10. Choice of the King's and Queene's Goldsmiths & Jewellers.

11. 20£ in gold, upon signing of the Goldsmiths Bill.

12. Lodgings in all ye King's Houses.

13. A close waggon (when ye Court removeth) for his owne goodes; and two carts for his officers.

14. Precedence in Courts & Kingdome.

15. Priviledg of the drawing roome.

16. Robes at the Coronation.

17. In Procession place before all the Judges.

18. He putteth on, and taketh off the King's Crowne.

19. He keepeth all the Regalia.

20. He hath lodgings etc. in y° Tower.

21. A servant there to keep y° Regalia.

22. He hath noe superior officer.

23. He fournisheth plate to Embassad™ and all the greate officers.

24. He remandeth it when Embassad™ returne ; & officers remove or dye.

25. He provideth a Garter & plaine George for Kn⁵ of y° Garter.

26. The total of his Retrenchm⁵ w°ʰ will serve to justify y° following preambe from vanity.

Note.—The above rights and perquisites were handed over by Sir H. Mildmay to Sir Gilbert Talbot in A.D. 1660.

Note.—These were the rights, privileges and emoluments of his predecessors, and Sir Gilbert Talbot goes on to relate how they had been curtailed and withdrawn.

Sʳ Gilbert Talbot entered into the service of K. Charles y° jˢᵗ at Venice an: 1637, and served his Maᵗʸ XI yeares first as Resident at 40ˢ. p. diem till the yeare 44, then as Envoye at 5£ per diem ; besides extraordinairies in both qualityes.

But by reason of the war, his Maᵗʸ was not able to send him any supply in soe much that he was forced to spend of his owne, and borrow of ye English and Dutch merchants to the value of 13000£ which his then Ma^{ty} promised to repay with ye interest wch hath since trebled ye principall.

But ye war still growing more obstinate and Sr G. Talbot not able to continue the expence begged leave of his M^{ty} to returne into England to represent his condition wch was graunted him for 6 moneths ; in Augst 44, he found the K^g at Bucannon and followed his Ma^{ty} in the Army ; till in 45 he was sent back to Venice, upon an extraordinary occasion ; with leave to returne when he should think fitt, because his Ma^{ty} was not yet able to maintain him abroad.

At his returne into England, in 46 his Ma^{ty} was pleased (a little before he went to the Scottish Army thus to recommend him to the Prince (now K^g).

Son here is a gentleman who hath served me faythfully many yeares ; and I have never bin able, hitherto, to doe anything for him. I therefore charge you to take notice of him & to see him well rewarded if I should not live to doe it myself.

The K^g going away to the Scotts ; the Prince into ye West, and Oxford surrendered Sr G. Talbot had his liberty upon those Articles. But the Pr : being forced to fly : the K^g sold into the

hands of the English : and afterwards barbar-
ously murdered ; Sir G. Talbot offered to goe
over to y⁰ p™sent King in Paris ; but was com-
manded to stay in London to corrispond with
Sʳ Robᵗ Long then Secretary, and to act for his
Maᵗʸᵉˢ service on this side of yᵉ water. For
wᶜʰ being afterwards discovered by Tom Cooke,
he was made close prisoner in Glocester ; and
there examined by Comifˢˢ upon 6 articles of
high Treason (as they were pleased to terme
them). But they having noe proofes to make
good any one article agˢᵗ him he had his liberty
upon bayle ; went over into France to his Maᵗʸ and
followed him in all his exile, till his restauration.

When every man (upon the prospect of his Maᵗʸⁿ
recall) was putting in for employment, Sʳ G.
T. ; by the assistance of the D. of Ormond,
obtained the graunt of Maister of the Jewell-
house forfeited by the treason of Sʳ Hen :
Mildmay and the reversion graunted by the
Martyr King to Sʳ Robᵗ Howard (brother of the
old E. of Berkshire) vacated by his death.

Upon his Maᵗʸⁿ returne Sʳ G. Talbot sent to Sʳ Hen :
Mildmay (at the time prisoner in Dover Castle)
to lett him understand that the Kᵍ had bestowed
the Jewell-house upon him ; and to know if he
would peaceably surrender his Patent ? he
returned answere That he could not give in the
patent because it lay buryed amongst many con-

fused papers But he was ready before a Maist^r of Chancery to make a formall resignation of the place which he accordingly performed

And promised moreover that if Sr G. T. would obteine from his Ma^{ty} a pardon of his life he would give him half his estate. Whereunto Sr G. T. reply'd that since he had soe freely resigned his office, he would endeavour to serve him, without any other condition : but desired him to send him a note of all the perquisites belonging to the place, wch he did and they are those wch are specifyed in ye jst page and shall hereafter be enlarged upon as they lye in order.

Sr G. Talbot's patent being passed (not wthout strong opposition from the Ld Chancell^r Hyde, who had shewed himself his enemy upon other occasions ; and had designed the Jewell-house for a Presbyterian friend) he took possession of his lodgings ; and entered upon the execution of his office.

When the Chancell^r found that he could not obstruct the patent, his next endeavour was to clip the profitts of the place, and therein his malice prevailed as will appeare when ye perquisites are treated of.

The perquisites belonging to ye M^r are as follows :

1. A Fee of 50£ per an payable half yearely out of the Exchequer : which ye Maist^r used to call for but

once in two yeares, that he might ioo£ together :
but when Sr George Downing became Secretary,
to the L^ds Commiss^n of the Treasury, he (because there is a small fee due to the Secretary
for drawing up the order to the Exchequer)
enioned[1] all fees to take out separate orders for
every half yeare : wch exacting invention is still
kept on foote : although the fee for every order
is exorbitant.

2. A Table of 14 double dishes per diem with bread
beer wine etc., or 35^s. per diem board wages, if
not served in kind. But ye Ld Chanc^r who
sought all occasions to preiudice the Maist^r of
the Jewell H. put the K^g upon retrenchm^t of
some of the tables : and went in person to the
Greenecloth (although altogether unqualifyed as
being noe Officer there) and cutt off the Maist^rs
table, and ye Groome-porters, for company,
that it might not look like personall malice ; in
lieu whereof they allowed each of them i2o£
p. an : board wages : and for this they plended
noe other ground, or shadow of reason, but
because it appeared in theyre books, that once
when the treasury was exhausted Sr H. Mildmay
proposed to the K^g the retrenchment of the
tables & desired his Ma^ty to begin with his.
This the Ld Chancell^rs Law, & Sr H. Woods
philosophy made an argument to cutt off the
dyet from the Jewell H.

[1] Enjoined.

And although Sr G. Talbot's patent gave him all the rights that any of his Predecessors at any time enioyed, there was noe releife to be had in theyre Chancery.

Sr G. Talbot this theyre proceeding to his Ma^{ty}, but the Chancellor yet swayed all things absolutely ; and there lay noe appeale from him.

For one yeare after they allowed him his dyet, at the greate Festivalls (Christmass, Easter, and Whitsontide) : but that was thought too much and retrenched likewise.

3. 300£ p. an : out of the money presented by the Nobility, to the King, at new-yeare's-tyde ; which usually amounted to 3000£. And the profitt ariss to the Maister by 12^d in the £, and the advantage of the gold ; for it was ever given away and payd in silver, till Mr. May came to the privy Purse, who gott it annexed to his office : by wch meanes that branch was cutt off from ye Maist^r of the Jewell H. because the K^s was neither to pay poundage, nor allowance for gold, and ye Maist^r had noe consideration for it, till upon the tender of severall petitions, his Ma^{ty} in an. 77 gave him, by Privy Seale 400£ p. an : out of the new-yeare's-guift money, during pleasure.

4. The Maist^r of the Jewell H. received the value of 300£ p. an. (coũunibg annis) by carrying presents to Embassadours, till the jst D. of

Buckingham (who was an enemy to Sᵣ H. Mildmay) prevailed wᵗʰ the Kˢ first, to make all his presents in iewells (and not in plate as had ever, till then, bin accustomed) and next to send them by the Maister of yᵉ Ceremonyes (an office erected but in Kˢ James his time).

Thus Sᵣ H. Mildmay (by his professed ignorance in iewels, had the buying of the iewels taken from the place, & usurped into the hands of the Lᵈ Chamberlan and the presenting of them, by his provocation of the D. of Buck : transferred to the Mᵣ of yᵉ Ceremonyes. Nay, and the keeping of all the private Jewells, is now in the hands of the page of his Maᵗʸˢ closet : although the Lᵈ Chamberlaine in what he buyeth, nor the sayd page in what he keepeth, hath any check upon him to controll the account of the one, or the guardianship of yᵉ other, whereas the account of the Jewell H. is under the inspection of the Lᵈ Treasurer, or a body of Comissⁿ when the K pleaseth to appoint them.

Thus while Sᵣ G. Talbot is Maister and Treasurer of his Maᵗʸᵉˢ iewells & plate, he is made a stranger to all but yᵉ Regalia, which alone is in his keeping.

v. The Maistᵣ of the iewell H. hath 28 ounces of gilt plate every new year : and the small presents wᶜʰ are sent to yᵉ Kˢ anciently valued at 30 or 40£ together with the purses wherein the Lords present theyre gold (wch were wont to be worth 30 or 40ˢ each. These the Ld Manchester (when Ld Chamberlaine) claimed as due to him : but Sr G. Talbot proved them to be his right : yet told his L^p that if he liked any of them he should have them, as a guift, not as a due.

The E. of St. Alban, who succeeded him, revived ye same pretence, but was opposed by the Maist^r and desisted. Yet usually the Maist^r gives the Ld Chamberl : 5 or 6 at the Cupboard, as he doth to other Officers & freinds y^t ask.

The profitt of allowance upon the ounces (issued out by guift from his Ma^ty) Sr G. T. gave (for his time) to his under Officers : and the carrying of presents to Resid^ts & Agents when made in plate, chaines or medals.

vi. Anciently the M^r of ye iewell H. was Treasurer of the Chamber, till that branch was taken over, and made an office apart : and is now five times more beneficiall than the iewell house : all the regulation of expence being applyed to the remaining parts of the perquisites of the iewell house ; the fees of ye treasur^r of the Chamber and M^r of y^e ceremonyes being left entire.

vii. The Maisters of the iewell H. have bin frequently privy Counsaillers, such was Crom- well [1] in y^e time of H. 8.   And appointed Ld Deputyes of Irel^d as the two Caryes.

viii. It belonged to the M^r of y^e iewell house to

_____
[1] Thomas Cromwell, Earl of Essex, temp. Henry VIII.

Q

buy, keep, & present all y⁵ iewells and plate that belonged to his Ma⁵ʸ but now that right is invaded, see number 4.

ix. The Maister hath the choice of all his inferior Officers ; and y⁵ power of suspending or displacing them upon their misbehaviours.

When he first took possession of his Office, he called to one of his Yeomen for the books which were in y⁵ keeping of old Layton, who then attended in his moneth ; the peevish old man who had lived long in y⁵ office refused to deliver them whereupon Sir G. Talbot shewed him the words of his patent ; but he remained obstinate and insolent & S⁵ Gilbert suspended him for waiting and acquainted his Ma⁵ʸ with it who very well approved of what he had done : but y⁵ passionate old man for very vexation of spirit dyed. His sonne had the impudence to claime his father's place ; and upon refusall to threaten an appeale to the K⁵ wherewith S⁵ G. Talbot acquainted his Ma⁵ʸ who sayd, if he came, he should receive an answere.

After this Serg⁵ Painter (without any application to S⁵ Gilbert) went boldly to the K⁵ and begged the reversion : and his Ma⁵ʸ graciously graunted it. Painter thus armed came to S⁵ Gilb⁵ and demanded to be admitted. S⁵ Gilbert asked whence he derived his claime ? he sayd : the K⁵ given it to him.

S⁵ Gilbert reply'd, he would receive y⁵ K⁵ pleasure

from himself ; and going to his Ma^ty asked him,
if he had appointed Painter to succeed Layton :
he sayd, yes. S^r, sayd Sr Gilb^t it belongeth to
me, to choose my owne Officers, because ye trust
of all ye Ma^ty^s plate is by me committed to them.
Well, sayd ye K. for this time let it pass, and I
will invade y^r right noe more. Sr Gilbert desired
to know if his Ma^ty would be security for all y^e
plate intrusted in his hands ? Noe indeed will I
not said the K^s and if that be requisite I recommend him not. S^r sayd Sr Gilbert this expostula-
tion is onely to show my right ; and ye danger
of admitting any without security : but since y^r
Ma^ty hath made choice of him, he shall stand,
and accordingly he admitted him.

x. The appointment of ye Goldsmiths and
Jewellers both to the K^s and Queene valued at
800£ each : (as the yeomens & Groomes places
are when vacant).

When his Ma^ty [1] came first into England Coronell
Blage (a groome of ye bedchamb^r) begged the
nomination of the Goldsmith & contracted w^th
alderman Backwell for 800£ but the alderman,
when he understood y^t it was the Maist^rs right,
quitted his bargaine & Mr Blage deserted his
pretension.

xi. The Maister used to receive 20£ in gold from
the goldsmith upon ye signing of his annuall bill :
(and this was transmitted in the list of perquisites

---

[1] King Charles II.

from Sr H. Mildmay to Sr G. Talbot ; yet would
he never require the same, least it might look like
a bribe to ye Maist^r to cast a favourable eye over
the account).

xii. He hath right to lodgings for himself, officers
& servants in all ye K^gs houses. Those in Whitehall were, when the K. came in, rude, dark &
intermixed with the Queene's servants.

The present dining roome was a kind of wild barne,
without any covering beside rafters and tiles.
The Maisters lodgings were two ill chambers,
above stayres, and the passage to them dark at
noone day ; his dining room was below. Sir
G. T. being desirous to improve his lodgings
proposed to his Ma^ty an exchange betwixt that
wilde roome, and his dining-roome. The K.
comanded the Ld Chamberl : to view, and
report wch he accordingly did : and told his
Ma^ty that S^r G^s proposall was fayre ; and much
to the advantage of the Queen's servants,
whereupon leave was given him to build ; and
when he had finished Sr E^d Wood came &
claimed his former lodging as being ye Q^s serv^t.
Sr Gilb^t told him he was ye K^gs servant, and had
built by his authority : and therefore presumed
he had good title to y^t apartment, and that the
. lower roome was his, if he pleased to like it, he
replyed had he would try his power ; and went

with a complaint agst S^r G^t to ye K^g who made
him answere that if he would not of the ground
roome, he should have none.   The angry K^t
finding the power of which he had boasted
fayle him, sayd :   he would then have none.
The K^g took him short at his word.   And S^r
Willm Throgmorton ye K^t Mareschall being by,
begged ye chamber, and enjoyed it for a yeare.
But ye nature of his place drawing greate con-
course of people thether, Sr G. thought it unsafe
for ye plate, represented ye danger to his Ma^{ty}
who thereupon caused the K^t Mareschall to be
warned out.   And least the chamber might draw
ill company againe he begged it for his Officers,
who have enjoyed it ever since.

xiii. Vpon all removalls of ye houshold the Maister
of the Jewell H. had ever a close waggon allowed
him :   for the transport of his servants and
goods :   and his officers had a waggon, and a cart
for the plate.

xiv. The M^r of ye Jewell H. was ever esteemed the
jst K^{nt} Bachelour of England and took place
accordingly.

He hath precedence of ye establishm^t of the household, before the Maist^r of ye greate Wardrobe :
and before ye Judges in all publeck processions
being ever next to the privy Counsaillers.

xv. They had the privilege to goe into the drawing
roome to the privy chamber where none beside

themselves, under the degree of Baron, were permitted to come, when yᵉ gallery was kept private.

xvi. At the Coronation they weare scarlet robes almost like yᵉ Barons robes, and dine at the Baron's table in Westminster Hall.

xvii. At the opening or concluding of a session of Parliament and at the passing of bills, when the K. appeareth in his robes the Mʳ of the Jewell H. putteth the Crowne upon his Maᵗʸᵐˢ head and taketh it off. And if he be absent or indisposed he deputeth a person of quality to doe it. And yᵉ Maister alone hath right to kneele at the steps below the Kᵍˢ feete (and yᵉ black Rod at yᵉ corner of the woolsack) although of late all yᵉ officers of the privy chamber and Presence (& by theyre example strangⁿ who have noe relation to the Court) take up theyre places there, and possess it all before the Maistʳ (who attendeth upon yᵉ Crowne) can come.

xviii. He keepeth all yᵉ Regalia (& the plate that is not used by the family) in the Tower and to that end had always convenient lodging for himself officers and servants therein.

In the new lodgings given in lieu of yᵉ old (because it was pretended yᵗ yᵉ chimneys might endanger the Magazin of powder which is lodged in the White Tower) there is not any appartement for

the Maister upon complaint thereof made by
Sr G. T. to the K. the matter was by his Ma^{ty}.
referred to ye consideration of ye Ordinance
board, how he might have his accommodation,
and ye officers of the board made Order that
there should be two new chambers built for him
upon the left hand of the open stayres by the
present Jewell house, which are of absolute
necessity to his Maties service, because in case
insurrection in the nation or tumult in the city
it is fitt the Maist^r should have his convenience
to watch over so considerable a charge.

xix. He hath a particular servant in the tower
intrusted with y^t greate treasure to whom
(because Sir G. T. was retrenched in all the
perquisites and profitts of his place as is above
specified) and not able to allow him a competent
salary, his Ma^{ty} doth tacitely allow that he shall
shew the Regalia to strangers, which furnisheth
him with soe plentifull a livelyhood, that Sir
G. T. upon the death of his servant there, had
an offer made him of 500 old broad pieces of
gold for the place.

Yet he first gave it freely to old Mr. Edwards (who
had bin his father's servant) whom Blud murdered, when he attempted to steale the crowne,
globe & scepter (as shall be related at large
hereafter).

After the death of the father he continued it to his sonne; and after his death he gave it to Maj^r Beckenham who maryed a daughter of old Edwards upon condition that he should maintaine old Mrs Edwards and ye children which he hath well performed.

xx. The Maister of the Jewell H. hath noe superiour Officer in Court over him. He receiveth noe command but from ye K^s himself wch is usually transmitted to him by warrant signed by the Ld Chamberlaine or other Secretary of State signifying the K^{rs} pleasure.

And many times he received it by word of mouth from his Ma^{ty} unless in case of greate importance wherein he usually desireth to have a warrant to be enterd for his iustification and indemnity.

Yet sometimes the Ld Treasurer or particular comĩss appointed for that end inspect the state of the Jewell H. as they did an. 1673 and '79.

xxi. The Maister of ye Jewell house fournisheth all the greate Officers of the household with plate; and all Embassad^{rs} that are sent abroad they giving indentures to restore the same, when called upon by him, and upon restauration he giveth back the indentures.

xxii. It is incumbent upon ye Maist^r to call upon all Embass^{rs} for theyre plate at theyre returne home; and upon the Executors of all greate officers who dye wth plate in theyre possession : and to sue in y^e Excheq^r any that are indebted to y^e Jewell house which debt cannot be privately compounded for by the Maist^r, but must be satisfyed by award of Court : or cancelled by y^e K$^{g's}$ pardon signified by privy Seale.

xxiii. If a knight of y^e Garter dye the Maister must send to his heyre or execut^r for his Collar, George & Garter wch his Ma^{ty} gave him at his installation :

and likewise to all serjeants for theyre Maces which are fournished out of the Jewell H.

xxiv. All the retrenchments of the perquisites belonging by Patent to Sr G. T. amount to 1300£ per an : which in 20 years since his Ma^{ty} came into England arise to 26000£.

Besides 13000£ original debt for his xi yeares service under the last K^g at Venice. Soe that if he had his right, there would be due to him 39000£ beside 26 or 27 yeares interest for the last sume of 1300£ expended in the Venetian service.

Sr G. Talbot Maister & Treasurer of the Jewell house.

May y^e 20th an : dom : 1680.

INDEX

250

CPSIA information can be obtained
at www.ICGtesting.com
Printed in the USA
BVHW041523050319
541836BV00008B/94/P